Lin-Manuel Miranda

From Broadway to the Big Screen

By Kristen Rajczak Nelson

Published in 2019 by
Lucent Press, an Imprint of Greenhaven Publishing, LLC
353 3rd Avenue
Suite 255
New York, NY 10010

Designer: Deanna Paternostro
Editor: Melissa Raé Shofner

Cataloging-in-Publication Data

Names: Rajczak Nelson, Kristen.
Title: Lin-Manuel Miranda: from broadway to the big screen / Kristen Rajczak
Nelson.
Description: New York : Lucent Press, 2019. | Series: People in the news |
Includes index.
Identifiers: ISBN 9781534563407 (pbk.) | ISBN 9781534563384 (library bound) |
ISBN 9781534563391 (ebook)
Subjects: LCSH: Miranda, Lin-Manuel, 1980–Juvenile literature. | Actors–United
States–Biography–Juvenile literature. | Composers–United States–Biography–
Juvenile literature. | Lyricists–United States–Biography–Juvenile literature.
Classification: LCC PN2287.M6446 R35 2019 | DDC 792.02'8092 B–dc23

Printed in the United States of America

CPSIA compliance information: Batch #BS18KL: For further information contact Greenhaven Publishing LLC, New York,
New York at 1-844-317-7404.

Please visit our website, www.greenhavenpublishing.com. For a free color
catalog of all our high-quality books, call toll free 1-844-317-7404 or fax
1-844-317-7405.

Contents

Foreword

We live in a world where the latest news is always available and where it seems we have unlimited access to the lives of the people in the news. Entire television networks are devoted to news about politics, sports, and entertainment. Social media has allowed people to have an unprecedented level of interaction with celebrities. We have more information at our fingertips than ever before. However, how much do we really know about the people we see on television news programs, social media feeds, and magazine covers?

Despite the constant stream of news, the full stories behind the lives of some of the world's most newsworthy men and women are often unknown. Who was Katy Perry before she was a pop music phenomenon? What does LeBron James do when he's not playing basketball? What inspires Lin-Manuel Miranda?

This series aims to answer questions like these about some of the biggest names in pop culture, sports, politics, and technology. While the subjects of this series come from all walks of life and areas of expertise, they share a common magnetism that has made them all captivating figures in the public eye. They have shaped the world in some unique way, and—in many cases—they are poised to continue to shape the world for many years to come.

These biographies are not just a collection of basic facts. They tell compelling stories that show how each figure grew to become a powerful public personality. Each book aims to paint a complete, realistic picture of its subject—from the challenges they overcame to the controversies they caused. In doing so, each book reinforces the idea that even the most famous faces on the news are real people who are much more complex than we are often shown in brief video clips or sound bites. Readers are also reminded that there is even more to a person than what they present to the world through social media posts, press releases, and interviews. The whole story of a person's life can only be discovered by digging beneath the surface of their public persona, and that is what this series allows readers to do.

The books in this series are filled with enlightening quotes from speeches and interviews given by the subjects, as well as quotes and anecdotes from those who know their story best: family, friends, coaches, and colleagues. All quotes are noted to provide guidance for further research. Detailed lists of additional resources are also included, as are timelines, indexes, and unique photographs. These text features come together to enhance the reading experience and encourage readers to dive deeper into the stories of these influential men and women.

Fame can be fleeting, but the subjects featured in this series have real staying power. They have fundamentally impacted their respective fields and have achieved great success through hard work and true talent. They are men and women defined by their accomplishments, and they are often seen as role models for the next generation. They have left their mark on the world in a major way, and their stories are meant to inspire readers to leave their mark, too.

Introduction

Bursting onto Broadway

Many playwrights and composers never see a show they have written make it to an Off-Broadway stage. Even fewer have seen their work in a Broadway theater. Lin-Manuel Miranda has done both—twice.

Miranda burst onto the Broadway scene at just 27 years old. He wrote and starred in *In the Heights*, which opened Off-Broadway in 2007 and moved to Broadway the following year. In 2015, *Hamilton: An American Musical* opened Off-Broadway at the Public Theater in New York City in January and swiftly moved to Broadway in July. It would go on to win an astonishing 11 Tony Awards, among many other honors, and sell out houses months ahead of time.

This success is no happy accident. Miranda has a rare combination of innate talent, work ethic, and creativity that is often described as "genius." While he would argue that timing and luck are part of the equation, the confidence others have placed in his capable hands shows it is more than that. Christopher Jackson, who starred with Miranda in both *In the Heights* and *Hamilton* has said, "It's easy to see his brilliance on a daily basis."[1]

Miranda's brilliance has been evident since his childhood. He attended a school for gifted children and graduated college with honors. Musical theater was part of his life very early on, too, with Broadway cast recordings of *Camelot* and other musicals spinning on the family record player. Though infrequently, Miranda had seen shows on the Great White Way of Broadway (the section of Broadway in New York City that makes up the theater district, named for the millions of lights making up the theatre marquees) while growing up. He also spent a good deal of time listening to many other genres of music, ranging from Disney movie music to salsa to hip-hop. Legendary Broadway composer John Kander told the *New York Times* that he calls Miranda "boy genius" and spoke on Miranda's gifts as a composer and lyricist: "Innovators are usually synthesizers—they synthesize everything they know and add their own personal talents, and out comes something new … What Lin is is a refreshing and healthy contemporary synthesist of everything he's known before."[2]

However, as Miranda listened to, wrote, and performed music as a young man, he started to become very aware that Broadway was, for the most part, the great *white* way. Miranda's family often spoke Spanish at home. His parents are both immigrants from Puerto Rico—and he did not see many people like himself on a Broadway stage. His contributions to the theater community are many, but perhaps one of the greatest is his commitment to diversity on stage. In addition, his charitable work speaking out about poor conditions in Puerto Rico today and fund-raising tracks, including the 2017 song "Almost Like Praying," truly add to the national conversation, not just the entertainment conversation.

The level of success Miranda has seen in his young career could easily go to his head. However, that is not Miranda. He continues to talk about working hard, following one's passions, and giving encouragement to the next generation of actors and playwrights. Perhaps his humble demeanor comes from the example set by his parents or his grandparents in Puerto Rico. It could be his roots in the Inwood neighborhood in New York City and growing up feeling like an outsider in the communities he was a part of. His humble demeanor could also come from the inherently risky ventures—and frequent failures—of musical theater writers. Whatever the reason, Miranda is a light for today's artists to look to. His story shows that no matter their ethnicity or age, any artist's story is worthy of being told if they have the time, courage, determination, and honesty to tell it.

Chapter One

Creative Beginnings

L in-Manuel Miranda was born January 16, 1980, in Inwood, a neighborhood found on the northernmost tip of the island of Manhattan in New York City. Though Manhattan is known for its bright lights and fancy stores, Inwood is found far from iconic landmarks such as the huge Macy's department store and the Empire State Building. When Miranda was born, the citizens of Inwood, including his parents, were largely Spanish-speaking immigrants.

Miranda's parents, Luis and Luz, came to New York City from Puerto Rico. Luis Miranda worked in politics, including as an adviser to New York mayor Ed Koch, who was in office throughout the 1980s. Dr. Luz Towns-Miranda, his mother, was a psychologist. Miranda's parents worked hard to set an example for him and his sister, also named Luz. "There was always something to be done, and they instilled that in us and so as we've gone on to our respective professions, we continue that legacy,"[3] Miranda said of his parents' work ethic. Since their parents worked full-time, Miranda and his sister were partly raised by another Puerto Rican native—their nanny, Edmunda Claudio. Claudio had also been Luis's babysitter when he was a child in Puerto Rico. Miranda called her *abuela*, which means grandmother in Spanish, partly because he does not

Miranda's parents, Luz (left) and Luis (right), have been married for more than 40 years.

remember his parents being around more than on weekends when he was young. "My dad and I would go and see an action movie, and then we would go and play Ping-Pong or pool. They were like weekend visits, even though we all lived in the same house,"[4] he said.

Gifted, but Lonely

Luis Miranda told *Smithsonian* magazine that his son was reading by about age three and that he would read to the other kids in his nursery school class. Then, at just six years old, Miranda took a special test and started school at Hunter College Elementary. Hunter is a free public school for smart, gifted children found on the wealthy Upper East Side of Manhattan. Children can only start school there in kindergarten, and they often go all the way through the school and graduate from high school there. Miranda

Early Tragedy

Though Miranda's childhood was mostly a happy one, something happened early in his life that affected him deeply. When Miranda was only four years old, his friend, also about four, drowned. He told *Rolling Stone* he remembers his parents telling him and the bus ride to school when she was not there. "I also remember sort of a year of gray,"[1] Miranda said. This experience brought him a sense of mortality, or understanding that people die, much sooner than most children. The knowledge would color how he saw life as he grew up and is unmistakable in his art.

1. Quoted in Brian Hiatt, "'Hamilton': Meet the Man Behind Broadway's Hip-Hop Masterpiece," *Rolling Stone*, September 29, 2015. www.rollingstone.com/culture/features/hamilton-meet-the-man-behind-broadways-hip-hop-masterpiece-20150929.

has spoken many times about what a great school he was able to attend. However, even as a very young child, he did not feel like he fit in anywhere.

First, he was one of the only Puerto Rican kids at Hunter. He took a bus from his mostly Latinx, Spanish-speaking neighborhood to an area of Manhattan that was primarily white and English speaking. He continued to speak Spanish at home and in his neighborhood, but only spoke English at school. Miranda recalls "code-switching," or switching from one language or way of speaking to another, between home and school as soon as he started kindergarten. His friends there called him "Lin," but at home he was called "Lin-Manuel." Miranda told NPR that he would visit friends on the Upper East and Upper West sides of Manhattan and translate for their Spanish-speaking nannies. "It's interesting to become a Latino cultural ambassador when you're 7,"[5] he said.

This experience also made Miranda feel out of place at his

Miranda's Puerto Rican heritage has deeply affected his whole life. In 2016, he was honored at the Puerto Rico Walk of Fame.

home in Inwood. He felt separate from the local kids who attended the neighborhood schools. He felt known as the kid who went to the special school. As far as Miranda knew, he was the only kid from his neighborhood to ever go to Hunter. This feeling of being left out of the community would continue into his teen years.

Miranda felt like an outsider in yet another place in his early life—Puerto Rico. He spent a month every summer there visiting his grandparents. However, he knew he was seen as the *gringo*, or an American who is not truly Latinx, and felt self-conscious of his Spanish, which was not quite as good as a native speaker's.

Getting on Stage

One place Miranda quickly felt at home was on stage. His father told the *New York Times* that at Miranda's first piano recital, he played a song that was followed by applause. "I remember his eyes popping up," Luis Miranda said. Miranda played another song, and another. "After the fourth round, the teacher gently pushed him off the piano so the other kids could play,"[6] Luis said.

In Puerto Rico

Miranda spoke at the Chicago Humanities Festival in 2016 about how important spending time in Puerto Rico was for him growing up. He said it showed him that Puerto Ricans can do any job they want—they can be doctors, lawyers, and more.

Furthermore, it connected Miranda to his roots and family in a special way. His grandparents let him do what he liked to do, which as a child was eat Starbursts, visit the arcade in San Juan, and make movies with a borrowed video camera.

His mother told *60 Minutes* that Miranda always loved to sing. "He was always creating and he loved words and songs."[7]

Though he did not continue his piano lessons, Miranda was able to foster this love for performing at Hunter. He was very conscious of how smart his classmates were. Because of this, he felt he needed to find what he was good at and work very hard to be the best at it. Music, theater, and performing were clear choices for him. As soon as he could, he started being part of school plays and musicals. One year in middle school, Hunter put on a series of musicals pared down to 20 minutes each. Miranda played a big part in these, appearing as Conrad Birdie in *Bye, Bye Birdie*, Captain Hook in *Peter Pan*, and Bernardo in *West Side Story*.

Some of these shows were already familiar to Miranda, who grew up listening to Broadway cast recordings. His mother would always listen to *Camelot,* and his father loved *The Unsinkable Molly Brown*. By his teen years, he had memorized dozens of shows, from *Jesus Christ Superstar* to *A Chorus Line*. His knack for memorizing lyrics would pay off in high school when he was cast as the Pirate King in *The Pirates of Penzance* and Judas in *Godspell*. As a senior, Miranda directed the school

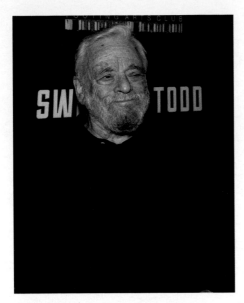

Broadway composer Stephen Sondheim wrote the lyrics for *West Side Story* and was a big influence for Miranda.

production of *West Side Story*. It was one time he brought his Latino background to Hunter. None of the young men in the cast were Latino, even though they were playing Puerto Ricans, so Miranda had his dad come in and help them with their accents.

That production of *West Side Story* brought about another important moment in Miranda's musical education: He met one of the show's creators, Broadway icon Stephen Sondheim. Sondheim knew the father of another student, and he came in and told the cast about writing the show. "It made an enormous impression," Miranda told the *New Yorker*. "It was the first time I had seen how a musical gets created for real."[8]

More Music

The musical backdrop of Miranda's life as he grew up was colorful, varied, and deep. In addition to Broadway musicals, the Miranda family listened to Latin music at home and danced salsa around the house. Miranda loved Disney movie musicals, too, especially *The Little Mermaid*. "I don't know why it changed my life as much as it did. I think Sebastian the crab had a big amount to do with it. The fact that this calypso number happens under the water just knocked my socks off,"[9] Miranda said of seeing the movie multiple times when it was released in theaters.

Perhaps the next biggest influence on Miranda was hip-hop. He credits his sister and a school bus driver for introducing him to the genre, as well as connected genres R&B (rhythm and blues) and rap. In sixth grade, he worked to learn all the lyrics to "The Choice Is Yours" by Black Sheep. He listened to Beastie Boys and Queen Latifah, and he got into his first and only fistfight over a copy of A Tribe Called Quest's album *Scenario* at age 13.

Not only did he find himself deeply entrenched in this eclectic mix of music, but he also felt compelled to share it. As a teenager, Miranda made mixtapes of all kinds of music for his friends, experimenting for the first time with combining seemingly opposing genres—Broadway and hip-hop. Later, he would realize the commonality that made him love both:

> *I fall in love with storytelling regardless of genre. Whether it's the new Aesop Rock album—"Blood Sandwich" is one of the best storytelling songs I've ever heard in hip-hop, full stop—or "A Weekend in the Country" from Sondheim's* A Little Night Music. *I love a well-told story in song.*[10]

Art in the Making

Growing up, Miranda spent a good deal of time creating his own stories and music, too. Some of this stemmed from feeling like he did not connect well with the other kids in his school. He started making movies, which put a VHS camcorder between himself and his peers. "I found it so much easier than actually talking to other kids. It's much easier to say, 'I'm making a movie, and I have a part for you' than 'Wanna hang out?'"[11] He even kept up his creative endeavors when he was visiting his grandparents in Puerto Rico. Miranda would use a surveillance camera borrowed from the credit union his grandfather worked at while at their house. He described the movies he made as "how a lonely kid keeps busy in Puerto Rico."[12]

The love of music in his life and the songs and performances Miranda sang and acted in started building toward something bigger as Miranda neared the end of high school. It seemed to gain steam when his girlfriend took him to see the musical *Rent* on Broadway for his 17th birthday in 1997.

Inspiration from McDonald's

Like many other teenagers, Miranda had a part-time job. One of his first jobs was working at McDonald's. Sometimes he worked at the counter, but he worked at a rare McDonald's that did delivery, which he much preferred. Later, he would use the experience to write a new song called "Delivery" for the revival of *Working*: "I'm off on a delivery/and I'm finally on my own/delivery, peace, and I'm heading to parts unknown/fresh air and exercise/and sometimes I throw in some extra fries."[1]

1. Ben Hewis, "Exclusive: First Listen to Lin-Manuel Miranda's 'Delivery' from *Working*," What's On Stage, May 24, 2017. www.whatsonstage.com/london-theatre/news/listen-lin-manuel-miranda-delivery-working-liam-tamne_43681.html.

Rent

In 2014, Miranda wrote a piece for the *New York Times* as a tribute to Jonathan Larson, the composer of *Rent*. Larson died in 1996, just months before *Rent* opened on Broadway. Miranda wrote of how deeply seeing the show influenced him, in part because of the diverse cast, something that was not common on Broadway stages. Before *Rent*, Miranda had seen less than a handful of shows on Broadway, and they were only the biggest shows out at the time: *Les Misérables*, *Cats*, and *The Phantom of the Opera*. These shows were all popular, famous, and traditionally featured entirely, or almost entirely, white casts. *Rent*'s time period changed how Miranda saw theater as well. He wrote that *Rent* was the first musical he had seen that took place in the present day. "More than anything," Miranda wrote, "[*Rent*] gave me permission to write about my community … 'Rent' whispered to me, 'Your stories are just as valid as the ones in the shows you've seen.'"[13]

Rent did not start Miranda writing about the Spanish-speaking

Miranda believed *Rent* changed how musical theater was made and what it could be about. Here, he is shown at its closing-night performance.

neighborhood he grew up in right away. However, it did start him writing. Miranda began to write one-act musicals about high school for his high school peers to perform in. One was called *Nightmare in D Major* and was about 15 minutes long. Another, *Seven Minutes in Heaven*, was about teenagers at a party. He even admits these first two musicals sound like *Rent*.

Miranda's parents fully supported his passion for these projects. However, they also wanted him to be able to take care of himself. To them, he was smart and creative, which meant he would be a great lawyer. Miranda did not really consider the idea: "I knew I was never going to be a lawyer. I knew that I wanted to make movies, and I wanted to write shows."[14]

Getting Schooled

After graduating from Hunter College High School in 1998, Miranda started school at Wesleyan University in Middletown, Connecticut. Living on campus proved to be an important moment of community building for Miranda. For his sophomore year, he wrote an essay about why he was a Latino community leader to earn a spot living in a Latino program house they called La Casa de Albizu Campos. Miranda found people who had similar experiences in the other Latino students living there. He later said he thought, "They've got the code switch down easy like I do."[15] Together, the community in La Casa de Albizu

Campos enjoyed the late 1990s boom of Latin pop music, including Enrique Iglesias, Ricky Martin, and Marc Anthony, who was previously known for singing only in Spanish. To Miranda, this moment in pop music felt significant: "I was figuring out these things about myself at the same time that the world was figuring out that we [Latinx] had something of value to offer, musically."[16]

Miranda started out at Wesleyan as a film and theater major, but as he started getting more involved with the theater community there, he dropped his film studies. He starred as Jesus in *Jesus Christ Superstar* and put on a version of *Seven Minutes in Heaven,* the short musical he wrote in high school. Wesleyan was a great follow-up to Hunter for Miranda, as he said at both places students "can find resources for whatever cockamamie [ridiculous] idea comes into your head."[17] Throughout his time there, he was writing new work. Looking back on his years at Wesleyan, Miranda told *Rolling Stone* he was "painfully aware" of how his parents were sacrificing for him to go to school: "I was not going to just leave with a B.A. [bachelor of arts degree] in something. I was going to leave with stuff. I wrote a show every year of college. Not for credit, but because I needed to be leaving with more than just a B.A."[18]

To the Heights

When home one summer from Wesleyan, Miranda worked as a writer for the *Manhattan Times*, a bilingual newspaper his father helped found. It reported on Inwood, as well as other communities in northern Manhattan, including parts of Harlem and Washington Heights. It was Miranda's job to report on the local happenings of the Washington Heights neighborhood, which helped him get to know it and its people very well.

As a sophomore, Miranda started to harness the music and experiences of growing up in his Spanish-speaking neighborhood in a musical. The first draft of *In the Heights* was an 80-minute, 1-act musical that blended Latin music and hip-hop, musical styles he had never written in before but loved deeply. It pulled from themes in *Rent* that resonated with Miranda—particularly, feeling like an outsider and finding a community of one's own. At this stage, *In the Heights* was based around a love triangle between Nina, who had left the neighborhood to go to a well-known college; Benny, who was not Latino; and Nina's brother Lincoln, who was romantically interested in Benny. Miranda has said this early version was a mix of all the musicals he had seen to that point.

When he finally put on the show, Miranda wanted the whole cast to be Latinx as the characters were written. He had to pull actors from all corners of campus, not just the theater department, to make this happen. Miranda, who performed in the show, said it was clear which songs made the audience sit up and listen: "This mix of Latin music and hip-hop was potent—there was something in that groove."[19]

Nonetheless, Miranda left *In the Heights* alone after it was performed on campus in 2000. His senior project was a musical called *On Borrowed Time*, and it was put on in 2002 at Wesleyan's Center for the Arts.

A few months later, Miranda graduated with honors from Wesleyan. He did leave with much more than a bachelor's degree. He had the beginning of something great with *In the Heights*—and it would not take him long to realize giving it a life after the Wesleyan stage was his calling.

Chapter Two

Reaching New Heights

Miranda moved back to New York City after college. His father recommended he go to law school so he would have a backup plan even if he wanted to continue trying to find his way in theater. However, Miranda had his sights set in a different direction—about 30 blocks downtown from home in Washington Heights.

Assembling the Team

Tommy Kail, who graduated a few years ahead of Miranda at Wesleyan, knew of Miranda by reputation. Kail had been given a recording of the college version of *In the Heights* and thought it had a lot of promise. He was interested enough in Miranda's work to go see his senior project *On Borrowed Time* and meet him, though Kail did not think the show was as good as *In the Heights*. Kail and a few other Wesleyan alumni had established their own theater company called Back House Productions in 2001. Shortly after, Kail and Miranda sat down to discuss *In the Heights*. The pair talked for 5 hours. "I had been thinking about 'In the Heights' for two years, and we started a conversation that never stopped,"[20] Kail said of that first meeting. Miranda said Kail started giving him notes on the show right away, including changing the song "In the Heights" to be the opening number and putting more focus on the character of Usnavi, which Miranda had played in the college production. Miranda took the ideas and ran with them.

Every few months after that, Miranda and Kail met to go over any new material Miranda had written. They brought in actors to read and sing through the parts, but Miranda always played Usnavi. "We couldn't find someone to learn all those raps, under an Equity contract, so I kind of fell in the snowball,"[21] he said.

Miranda has said it is clear that both he and Kail have made their best work when working together.

Making Ends Meet

While working hard on *In the Heights*, Miranda had to work other jobs, including writing jingles for clients of his father. He took a job as a substitute teacher at Hunter, his old school. Miranda felt he was only just keeping up with the students in the seventh grade English classes he taught.

Eventually, Hunter asked him to stay on as a part-time teacher. At this point, *In the Heights* was starting to be noticed by producers. Jill Furman, Kevin McCollum, and Jeffrey Seller—all veteran Broadway producers with Tony-winning shows on their resumes—started to show interest in funding the new musical.

Freestyle Love Supreme

When Miranda was not working on *In the Heights*, he was performing with his hip-hop improvisation comedy group, Freestyle Love Supreme. The group—which featured Miranda, as well as Tony-winner James Monroe Iglehart and Tony-nominee Christopher Jackson—would eventually perform all over the world. Their TV series aired on Pivot TV in 2014.

Miranda and other members of Freestyle Love Supreme would use audience suggestions to write improvised rap and musical numbers.

They knew it was risky to bet on a new playwright and composer—but it was a risk that could really pay off.

Diving into *In the Heights* full-time was risky for Miranda, too, so he asked his father for advice. Luis wrote him a letter, telling his son that though it made no sense for him to leave his job to pursue writing, he was going to tell Miranda to do it anyway.

Tackling the Story

Kail and Miranda worked on *In the Heights* together for quite

The Birth of a
Broadway Musical

While there are many ways for a new musical to reach Broadway, one common path is similar to the route taken by *In the Heights*:

Step 1: A show is conceived of and partially or mostly written.

Step 2: The show has workshops, or opportunities for actors to read and sing the parts, sometimes in front of an audience. After a workshop, the story and dialogue, called the "book," and songs are revised.

Step 3: Producers offer money to support more workshops or a staging at a theater.

Step 4: The show is produced at a small theater, perhaps at a regional or Off-Off Broadway theater. Off-Off Broadway theaters are smaller than 99 seats, and the cast and crew are often paid very little. The show continues to be revised.

Step 5: The show is produced Off-Broadway, which means everyone in the cast is paid and the show is performed in theaters that have fewer than 500 seats. Some shows do runs in big theater cities other than New York, such as Chicago, Illinois, and Washington, D.C.

Step 6: The show moves to Broadway.

These steps can take many years or happen fairly quickly—it all depends on the show.

awhile when it was becoming more and more obvious to them both that Miranda could not handle every task he had. He was composing the music, writing the lyrics, and performing in *In the Heights*. The book needed more help than he could manage. They found the perfect writing partner in Quiara Alegría Hudes. Hudes was also raised with Puerto Rican parents in a mostly Latinx neighborhood in Philadelphia, Pennsylvania. When she started working on *In the Heights*, Hudes, at just 25, was of a similar age to Miranda and Kail, too.

Since working with Miranda, Quiara Alegría Hudes has won a Pulitzer Prize for Drama for a play called *Water by the Spoonful*.

Hudes began to focus *In the Heights* on the neighborhood as a whole, instead of it simply being a love story. She made cuts to the stories in the show and continued with Kail's original suggestion: She made Miranda's character, Usnavi, a bigger part of the story. Usnavi became the narrator and the lens through which much of the story of the neighborhood was told. "It's not every day you write a part for yourself and people say, 'Yeah, that's great. Do it,'" Miranda said on the PBS episode of *Great Performances* dedicated to *In the Heights*. "So I'm trying to just enjoy that as much as I can."[22]

As they wrote, Miranda said they looked to great, well-known musicals for inspiration. He mentioned *Fiddler on the Roof*, another portrait of a community, as one that was particularly important in the writing of *In the Heights*. He added that the song "Tradition" in *Fiddler on the Roof* introduced a community to the audience the best way a show could.

Inspiration came from a much more personal place for both

Miranda and Hudes, too. Looking back on the writing of *In the Heights*, Miranda has said the show was a "love letter to our families,"[23] and that they both drew from their lives to create the scenes and characters of the show. Hudes left her Latinx neighborhood for a prestigious school when she went to college at Yale University, just like Nina who leaves Washington Heights for Stanford University. One line in particular stands out to Miranda as reflective of his own life:

> I think one of the most autobiographical sections of the show is Nina's bridge in "When You're Home": "When I was younger I'd imagine what would happen if my parents had stayed in Puerto Rico." That line is like what I spent most of my childhood wondering. That question of finding home is not only a geographical one, but really an emotional one. What does it mean to be Puerto Rican if you don't live in Puerto Rico? Or Dominican if you don't live in the Dominican Republic?[24]

"Hundreds of Stories"

In *In the Heights*, Miranda and Hudes wanted to give more realistic, rounded portrayals of Latinx characters, something Miranda felt was missing from musicals: "There should be a show with Latino people where we aren't gang members and drug dealers, because that's been super well represented already."[25] The cast, many of whom came from Latinx families and heritages, told PBS the show truly expressed their families' experiences in a special way. One cast member, Robin De Jesus, echoed the need for fairer portrayals of their ethnicities: "Finally a role where I'm not in a gang, I'm not carrying a gun, I'm not selling drugs. I'm just a normal human being who happens to be Hispanic and happens to live in this wonderful place called Washington Heights."[26]

Many colorful barrio residents added depth to the portrayal of Washington Heights—from the older woman born in Havana, Cuba, who everyone calls *abuela* to those who work and gossip in the hair salon to the young idealist who wants to make life

In the Heights featured many Latinx and Hispanic actors as the multi-ethnic barrio residents.

better in the neighborhood. The characters of *In the Heights* wrestle with their pasts and identities, particularly as Latinx Americans, and consider their futures and what their legacies might be. They worry about gentrification (the renovation of a deteriorating area or house so it conforms to higher standards yet leaves poor people without a home) changing their neighborhood as storefronts are taken over by nonresidents, and they sing about all of it. "I think it's accurate, but you know, it's a musical," Miranda told the *New York Times* in 2008. "I think most people think of Washington Heights as the place where Jay-Z goes uptown to get his drugs processed in his songs … That wasn't my reality growing up."[27]

The main story of *In the Heights* centers around a few key characters:

Usnavi: A Dominican bodega, or small grocery store, owner who dreams of returning to the Dominican Republic where his deceased parents were from.

Vanessa: A barrio resident not content with her life there

and wishing to escape for bigger things downtown or away from New York City completely.

Nina: A college student at Stanford University returning home unsure of what her path should be going forward.

Benny: A black, non-Latinx young man working in the barrio, longing for the money to go to business school and work for himself.

They have families, dreams, and fears that are tied to their roots and the barrio.

Many of the young people in the show—like the cast and some of the creators—are first-generation Americans. They, like Miranda, are grappling with how that fits into their lives. "You grow up with your parents' tradition, you go to school with a completely different set of traditions, and you try to find yourself within the margins. I certainly have. I've tried to write a show working that out for myself,"[28] Miranda told PBS. However, to state that *In the Heights* is only about the Latinx American experience is selling it short. The characters' ethnic identity is only one part of their story. Their experiences are also universal, including worries about fitting in and disappointing family.

Making It to Off-Broadway

Miranda and Hudes continued to fine-tune the book, lyrics, and score through workshops at the Manhattan Theater Club, a stay at the Eugene O'Neill Theater Center in Connecticut, and even more workshops. Years into the process, *In the Heights* was coming together, but the long road was difficult. Miranda wrote in 2014 that seeing the musical *Tick, Tick... Boom!*, the story of a struggling songwriter in New York, when he was 21 gave him a glimpse at what the life in musical theater might be like: "Readings and workshops going nowhere, jobs allowing only flexible hours, relationships ending because the writing comes first and must always come first,

Latinx or Hispanic?

Miranda often describes himself as "Latino." The term "Latinx," which is a gender-neutral term used instead of Latino or Latina, can be used to describe the ethnicity of someone from Latin America. This includes all of South and Central America, as well as Mexico, Puerto Rico, the Dominican Republic, and Cuba. It is sometimes used interchangeably with the term "Hispanic," which refers to people who come from a Spanish-speaking country, but the labels have some differences. Someone from Spain, for example, is Hispanic but not Latinx. Someone from Brazil is Latinx, but not Hispanic because Brazil's major language is Portuguese.

watching talented friends adjust their dreams and find happiness in other careers with more stability. Every young artist deals with these realities."[29]

Through these struggles, Miranda was still inspired by Washington Heights. If he was having a hard time creating something in the show, he would drive to a park in the neighborhood. He loved it so much, he told the *New York Times* he wanted to move there when he could afford it.

All of Miranda's time and energy began to pay off when it was announced that a full production of *In the Heights* would open Off-Broadway at a theater called 37 Arts in early 2007. The cast, some of who had been part of the show since it was in workshops, included Tony-winner Priscilla Lopez, Andréa Burns, Mandy Gonzalez, Karen Olivo, Christopher Jackson, and Miranda, who would continue playing Usnavi. Kail signed on to direct the show, and he and Miranda brought in choreographer Andy Blankenbuehler to add movement, an important part of both Latin music and hip-hop culture. Alex Lacamoire served as the music director. Previews of the show started January 9, and

Learn Spanish from
In the Heights

In the Heights is mostly in English, but there are many Spanish words included and several Spanish phrases repeated throughout the show. Sometimes, the Spanish is translated within a song, such as in the exchange between Benny and Nina in "Sunrise." Here are some other translations not included in the show:

Spanish	English
barrio	neighborhood
café	coffee
paciencia y fe	patience and faith
alabanza	praise
Esa bonita bandera contiene mi alma entera.	That pretty flag contains my whole soul.
¡No me diga!	You don't say!
sigue, sigue	follow, follow
no pare	don't stop
¡Ay dios mio!	Oh, Lord!

The first U.S. performances of *In the Heights* performed primarily in Spanish took place in Washington, D.C., in April and May 2017.

the show officially opened February 8.

Reviews of the show were positive, though some thought it still needed a bit more work, especially Act Two. Reviews of Miranda, though, were glowing. The *New York Times* praised his musicianship: "The emotional heart of the show is the ambivalence most of the characters feel about their neighbor-hood—and their lives—and this uncertainty is given powerful expression in Mr. Miranda's songs."[30] *New York* magazine called the score Miranda wrote "rich and kaleidoscopic" and stated his lyrics were "some of the best that New York has heard from a young songwriter since *Avenue Q*."[31]

By May, the producers had announced *In the Heights* would open on Broadway the following year. It closed Off-Broadway on July 15, 2007, to take the needed time to refine and revise the show for Broadway. At 37 Arts, it played 33 preview perfor-mances and 181 regular performances.

Taking the Broadway Stage

The set of *In the Heights* is based on the actual neighborhood of Washington Heights. It included Usnavi's bodega, with real candy and other products for sale, the hair salon, and street-lights. Miranda and Kail walked through Washington Heights with the set designer while they were conceiving the set for the Off-Broadway production of the show. As they moved it to the historic Richard Rodgers Theatre, Miranda marveled on PBS's

Miranda made his Broadway debut with *In the Heights*.

Great Performances that it was surreal to see his neighborhood inside it.

In the Heights opened for previews February 14, 2008, and officially opened March 9, 2008. At the curtain call on opening night, Miranda looked excited and emotional. As he took his bow, he reached for a microphone and addressed the crowd: "I don't ever want to forget this moment as long as I live. Ay, Mama, what do you do when your dreams come true?"[32]

The *New York Times* review by critic Charles Isherwood again focused on Miranda:

> *The theater has not gone out of the star-making business entirely. If you stroll down to the Richard Rodgers Theater, where the spirited musical "In the Heights" opened on Sunday night, you'll discover a singular new sensation, Lin-Manuel Miranda, commanding the spotlight as if he were born in the wings.*[33]

The Awards Kept Rolling In

On May 13, 2008, just two months after *In the Heights* opened on Broadway, it received the most Tony Award nominations of any show that season at thirteen. The nominations included Best Book of a Musical for Hudes, Best Performance by a Featured Actor in a Musical for De Jesus, Best Performance by a Featured Actress in a Musical for Olga Merediz, Best Direction of a Musical for Kail, Best Choreography for Blankenbuehler, and Best Orchestrations for Lacamoire and Bill Sherman. It was also nominated for Best Scenic Design of a Musical, Best Costume Design of a Musical, Best Lighting Design of a Musical, and Best Sound Design of a Musical.

Miranda was nominated for two Tony Awards for his work on *In the Heights*—Best Original Score and Best Performance by a Leading Actor in a Musical. The show was also nominated for what is often the last award of the night, Best Musical.

With this final nomination, the cast was set to perform at the 2008 Tony Awards. Miranda was introduced by Whoopi Goldberg and started the performance off with his opening number rap "In the Heights." The cast quickly flooded the stage, set as the barrio, and transitioned into show highlight "96,000." The performance was a showstopper, showing millions of viewers watching on television what New York theatergoers had been excited about for months.

In the end, *In the Heights* won Tony Awards for Best Orchestrations and Best Choreography. Miranda won his first Tony Award for Best Original Score. He beat out composer Alan Menken and the lyricists from *The Little Mermaid*—a shock for Miranda, who had loved the movie as a child. He performed a rap for his acceptance speech:

I used to dream about this moment, now I'm in it!

Tell the conductor to hold the 'ton a minute

I'll start with Alex
Lacamoire and
Bill Sherman

Kevin McCollum,
Jeffrey Seller and
Jill Furman

Quiara for keeping the
pages turning

Tommy Kail for
keeping the
engine burnin'

For bein' so discernin'
through every
all nighter

Dr. Herbert for tellin'
me "you're a writer"

Miranda's acceptance speech at the 2008 Tony Awards was improvised.

I have to thank Andy Blank for every spank.

Matter fact thank John Bizetti for every drink.

Thank the cast and crew for having each other's backs

I don't know about God but I believe in Chris Jackson.

I don't know what else I got, I'm off the dome

I know I wrote a little show about home

Mr. Sondheim, look, I made a hat

Where there never was a hat!

It's a Latin hat at that!

Mom, Dad and Cita, I wrote a play,

Y'all came to every play

Thanks for being here today

Vanessa who still makes me breathless

Thanks for lovin' me when I was broke and makin' breakfast

And with that, I want to thank all my Latino people

This is for Abuela Risa in Puerto Rico

Thank you.[34]

In the Heights also won one of the biggest awards of the night for Best Musical. It would go on to win the 2009 Grammy Award for the original Broadway cast album of the show, too. It was then a finalist for the 2009 Pulitzer Prize in Drama. When In the Heights opened in London, England, in 2016, Miranda won an Olivier Award for Outstanding Achievement in Music for the production.

Latinx Prejudice

Miranda told *Rolling Stone* that prejudice toward Latinx people is very real. He said he experienced prejudice often growing up. Even with the success of *In the Heights*, he was mistaken for a waiter more than once at black-tie events: "I was at a thing and a lady waves me over and goes, 'She never got her salad.'"[1]

This prejudice can lead to fewer opportunities for Latinx people, Miranda said. He quickly learned that if he wanted to play a lead in something, he would have to write it himself.

1. Quoted in Brian Hiatt, "'Hamilton': Meet the Man Behind Broadway's Hip-Hop Masterpiece," *Rolling Stone*, September 29, 2015. www.rollingstone.com/culture/features/hamilton-meet-the-man-behind-broadways-hip-hop-masterpiece-20150929.

Finale

Miranda stayed in the cast of *In the Heights* for about a year, leaving the role of Usnavi on February 15, 2009. With the announcement of his departure, *Playbill* said, "Miranda's rapid-fire rap delivery, puppy-dog charm and kinetic energy made his work stand out in the 2007-08 season."[35] He would return as Usnavi for the final two weeks of the show's run before it closed January 9, 2011.

Miranda knows how momentous writing and starring in the show was in his life: "The success of *In the Heights* gave me a life as a writer, a career as a writer, it said, 'You belong here.' Nothing will ever do for me what that show did—from broke to not broke—in every respect."[36]

In the Heights opened the door for Miranda on Broadway, but it also showed that diversity can be part, and even an integral part, of a hit Broadway show. Furthermore, it broadened the genre of a Broadway musical to include more Latin music and hip-hop. The boundary between rap, hip-hop, R&B, and traditional Broadway scores started to blur with Miranda's music in *In the Heights*—but it still existed for some people: "When *Heights* came out, there was a lot of 'Hip-hop on Broadway?' The same way you got 'Rock on Broadway?'"[37] For Miranda, that boundary would soon blur so far that it might disappear completely.

Chapter Three

From One Great Project to the Next

It took seven years for *In the Heights* to make it from a college musical to Broadway—and Lin-Manuel Miranda was at the helm of it every step of the way. Though the outcome was a success he was grateful for, the process was tiring. When he finally took a vacation from the show in 2008, he and his girlfriend, Vanessa Nadal, went to a resort in Mexico. It was then that his next original idea came to him. As Miranda told *Huffington Post*: "The moment my brain got a moment's rest, 'Hamilton' walked into it."[38]

Beach Read

Before heading on vacation, Miranda had picked up a book to read. He chose author Ron Chernow's 2004 book *Alexander Hamilton*, an 800-plus page tome chronicling the rise of Founding Father Alexander Hamilton from poverty to the first Secretary of the Treasury. Shortly into reading the book, Miranda had a revelation: The life of Alexander Hamilton had a hip-hop arc to it. He later said that by the second chapter, he knew the book was his next show.

Hamilton, like many hip-hop artists, had a hard childhood. He was born on the island of Nevis to a Scottish father and

British West Indian mother. His father left the family early, and his mother fell ill and died when Hamilton was about 13. Hamilton went to live with a cousin, but the cousin committed suicide. When Hamilton was a teenager, a hurricane hit his island. He wrote a letter to his father about it, and money was raised to send him to the British colonies for a formal education.

The way Miranda saw it, "He literally wrote his way out of his circumstances," just like JAY-Z, Eminem, or Lil Wayne. "Having had that insight very early while reading Ron Chernow's book, I never pictured the literal Founding Fathers again."[39]

Not long after, Miranda invited Chernow to see *In the Heights.* Christopher Jackson remembered how Miranda responded to the author being there: "I had never seen Lin that nervous. He said, 'Ron Chernow's here!' I said, 'What does that mean?' And he said, 'The show needs to go well today.'"[40]

Miranda asked Chernow to be the historical consultant on the project that day. Chernow said Miranda

Ron Chernow (left) was one of the first people to hear Miranda rap about Alexander Hamilton. Miranda did it for Chernow in his living room.

Ron Chernow on Miranda

Ron Chernow was quite involved with the writing of *Hamilton*. He told *Playbill* that at first he just told Miranda about errors, and then he later helped with ideas about characters' portrayals. He would see the show at every workshop or staging to keep it as historically on track as was necessary. "Lin was a strong enough personality with a sense of integrity that allowed him to really have the biographer deeply involved in this way,"[1] Chernow said.

1. Quoted in Janice C. Simpson, "The Man Who First Brought Us *Hamilton*—Ron Chernow on Serving as Lin-Manuel Miranda's 'Right Hand Man,'" *Playbill*, January 12, 2016. www.playbill.com/article/the-man-who-first-brought-us-hamilton-u2014-ron-chernow-on-serving-as-lin-manuel-mirandas-right-hand-man.

told him he wanted to make sure the history was right as he wrote so it would be something real historians could take seriously. "This story is more delicious and tragic and interesting than anything I could have made up,"[41] Miranda said of the story of Hamilton as Chernow relayed it in his book. Chernow's feedback became part of the writing process.

Spanish, on the West Side

While still performing in *In the Heights*, Miranda started working with a Broadway big shot: Arthur Laurents. Laurents is best known for writing the librettos, or the text of a vocal work, of *West Side Story* and *Gypsy*. Laurents's partner, Tom Hatcher, had seen a Spanish-language production of *West Side Story* and suggested Laurents put on a Broadway version that used the native language of the Puerto Rican characters. Laurents took this suggestion and called Miranda to work on making the show more bilingual. Miranda—recommended by Kevin McCollum, who was a producer on both *In the Heights* and the *West Side Story* revival—was only given one boundary to work within. The original lyricist, Stephen Sondheim, asked that the Spanish translation keep the rhyme schemes for English-speaking listeners. "It was the hardest bilingual crossword puzzle I've ever done,"[42] Miranda told the *New York Times*.

Miranda spent a lot of time at his parents' apartment in Inwood while trying to sort out translations that would rhyme and reflect the kind of Spanish the Sharks (one of the gangs in the story, led by Bernardo) would be speaking. For help, Miranda went to his father, who was a Spanish-speaking Puerto Rican living in New York City at the time portrayed in *West Side Story*. Spanish was added throughout the show, but Miranda worked on two iconic songs in particular, translating them almost completely into Spanish. "I Feel Pretty" translated to "Siento Hermosa," and "A Boy Like That/I Have a Love" became "Un Hombre Así/I Have a Love."

After *West Side Story,* Karen Olivo (left) took a break from Broadway. However, Miranda helped draw her back to New York in 2014 for a production of *Tick, Tick...Boom!* starring Miranda and Leslie Odom Jr.

As Miranda translated *West Side Story*, the show was being cast, a process he was part of. Karen Olivo, the big-voiced actress playing Usnavi's love interest, Vanessa, in the original cast of *In the Heights*, won the role of Anita. Though he was sad to lose her from *In the Heights*, Miranda had to be thrilled to have such a powerhouse vocalist in another show he was part of. In fact, Olivo would be the standout in the revival, both receiving glowing reviews and a Tony Award for Best Featured Actress in a Musical.

The Spanish translations of the show, however, received less favorable notices. Ben Brantley at the *New York Times* asked, "Since music is supposedly a universal language (and since the Jets and Sharks often sing the same melodies), do we have to have key, plot-propelling songs translated (by Lin-Manuel Miranda) into Spanish as well?"[43] Brantley proposed that viewers new to the show might have a hard time figuring out what was happening in the second act if they did not speak Spanish. Nonetheless, the revival played for 27 previews and 748 regular performances, and the cast album won a Grammy Award in 2010 for Best Musical Show Album. It closed on Broadway January 2, 2011.

White House Workshop

Soon after *West Side Story* opened on Broadway in March 2009, Miranda was invited to "An Evening of Poetry, Music, and the Spoken Word" at the White House, hosted by President Barack Obama and First Lady Michelle Obama. Miranda was asked to perform something from *In the Heights*, which he had just left, or something relating to the American experience. He decided to swing for the fences and perform an early song from *Hamilton*. On *Late Night with Seth Meyers*, Miranda said he did not even have a whole song written at that point: "I'd written sixteen hot bars about *Hamilton*."[44]

At the time, few people had heard parts of the *Hamilton* project. One was Alex Lacamoire, the co-orchestrator on *In the Heights*. He told the Broadway Backstory podcast that Miranda showed him the part of "Alexander Hamilton" to play on piano and then rapped over it. Lacamoire said of Miranda sharing the early music: "Most of the time Lin is just so excited to share what he's written …which is wonderful … it takes a lot of vulnerability, you know, you expose yourself a lot when you show something you've written."[45] Miranda asked Lacamoire to perform with him at the White House.

Their performance of "Alexander Hamilton" got a big reaction from the audience assembled, including from the

The official YouTube video of Miranda performing at the White House in 2009 has been viewed more than 5 million times. President Barack Obama is shown here at the event.

president and First Lady. However, it also went viral online. Miranda told Seth Meyers that the top comment on YouTube for a long time was that commenters' history teachers were showing the clip. It was clear already that Miranda had hit on something special. Oskar Eustis, artistic director of the Public Theater in New York City, was stunned by the White House video. He knew right away that Miranda had an amazing concept. Eustis immediately began trying to persuade Miranda to make his project a musical and put it on at the Public. However, Miranda insisted the project, to him, was a concept album.

Best of Wives, Best of Women

Miranda was on a professional roll by the end of the 2009; it was time to focus on his personal life. Around Halloween 2009, he and his long-time girlfriend, Vanessa Nadal, were engaged in Madrid, Spain, where they were vacationing.

Nadal grew up in Washington Heights and had been a few years behind Miranda at Hunter College High School. They did not get to know each other until they were both in their 20s. During the summer of 2005, Miranda invited Nadal to a Freestyle Love Supreme event via Facebook. A few weeks later, they were dating. They were together while he took *In the Heights* from the 80-minute, 1-act play to Broadway, and he thanked her in his Tony acceptance speech. Nadal had an equally busy life while Miranda was putting up the show. She decided to change career paths after graduating from college with a degree in chemical engineering and went to law school to become a lawyer. She finished school in the spring of 2010. She and Miranda were married on September 5, 2010.

Before becoming a lawyer, Nadal worked as a scientist at Johnson & Johnson.

A group of Broadway singers performed at their wedding ceremony. However, that was not the only performance. Miranda surprised his new wife with a choreographed version of "To Life" from *Fiddler on the Roof* featuring his father, father-in-law, Tommy Kail, other members of the bridal party, and guests.

Even celebrating such a personal milestone, Miranda's mind was at work. While on his honeymoon with Nadal, he wrote a song for King George to sing in the *Hamilton* project. When they returned home, he learned that *In the Heights* was closing. It was time to find the next big thing.

Art and the Process

Miranda was a man in demand. After *In the Heights*, he "pitched every Latin-themed anything that was coming from anywhere."[46] He told *New York Times* that he had a folder on his computer called "Post-Heights," and everyone wanted to know what was in it. Miranda was determined not to let anyone know what his next move would be. He looked into writing a musical based on the books *Team of Rivals* and *My Name Is Asher Lev*. Neither came to be, but he was not upset: "I don't need to tell every story. I just have to chase what I'm passionate about."[47]

Still, he felt the ticking clock of age and time, something that had stayed with him since he was a child. "I'm very aware that an asteroid could kill us all tomorrow. But I create works of art that take years and years to finish. So it's an enormous act of faith to start a project."[48] He had some work done for the *Hamilton* project, but he was not sure what it was yet. Miranda thought it might be a concept album he was thinking of calling *The Hamilton Mixtape*.

Using the word "mixtape" harkened back to Miranda making mixes for girls in high school. He told author Michael Chabon that the name *The Hamilton Mixtape* was autobiographical and likened making a mixtape to his creative process of writing a show: "You're gonna rise and you're gonna fall, then you're gonna slow it down, then you're gonna speed it up, and all of the lyrics have secret meanings to you that you're trying to transmit to the person you are giving it to."[49]

Miranda has often reported writing songs while riding the subway or walking his dog. "I will write eight or sixteen bars of music I think is exciting, or interesting, or sounds like the pulse of the character I want to be speaking, and then I will go and put on my headphones and walk my dog and talk to myself,"[50] he told the *New Yorker*. He will sometimes record himself as he goes using the voice-memo feature of his phone. He said this is exactly how he wrote "Wait For It," a major character song for *Hamilton*: He started singing the melody on the way to a birthday party, recording with his iPhone. He only stayed at the party for 15 minutes—he left to write the rest of the song on the train ride home.

The writing for the *Hamilton* project was slow for a few years.

In that time, he tackled a project that to an outsider's view would seem out of place—but Miranda had good reason to do it:

> We write musicals, and one out of five shows that reaches Broadway makes its money back. That's a four out of five failure rate in terms of seeing a return on your investment. So, what is the lesson you take away from that? You cannot do something because you think it will make money ... You have to do it because you believe in it and you have to do it because you love it. Or, you have to do it because you believe you will learn from it.[51]

Learning from the Best

In 2009, Andy Blankenbuehler, the choreographer from *In the Heights*, came to Miranda and told him he would be working on a musical version of *Bring It On*, a cheerleading movie franchise first released in 2000. The idea of making a musical adaptation of the movie or its sequels did not appeal to Miranda at all. That was until he heard that Jeff Whitty, who was writing the book for the show, had a concept in mind. Miranda trusted Whitty, who had won a Tony Award for his book for the blockbuster musical *Avenue Q*. Whitty wanted the musical's story to be drawn from *All About Eve*, but with cheerleaders. *All About Eve* is a famous movie from 1950 in which a woman inserts herself into the life of an actress and her friends to get ahead as an actress herself. Miranda was intrigued, but concerned about writing the whole score himself. Once again, the team behind *Bring It On* eased his fears. He would be sharing the score-writing duties with Tom Kitt, the composer of the Tony Award and Pulitzer Prize winning *Next to Normal*. Miranda told Grantland about the learning experience of being part of *Bring It On*:

> It was never in my soul and bones to write a musical about cheerleading. But I knew I'd learn a lot watching Andy [Blankenbuehler] direct and writing with Tom [Kitt], who to me

Working with the creative team for *Bring It On,* shown here, made Miranda an even better collaborator, setting him up for success as he worked on his next projects.

> *is one of the best melodists of our generation. Watching him think through an idea and see it go through his filter—it was like,* Oh, I'm going to learn some moves.[52]

At first, it was planned that Miranda and Kitt would write songs somewhat separately, roughly dividing the music between the rival schools featured in the plot. Kitt would write the pop songs, and Miranda would work on the hip-hop. That did not last, and for the most part, the score was a collaborative process in which some songs' melodies were written by Miranda and some by Kitt. Miranda and Amanda Green both wrote lyrics. Miranda wrote one song, "One Perfect Moment," while staying in his teen-age bedroom, writing all night as if in a diary. Miranda loved the team effort: "The fact that this was a composing team means that I couldn't have written this by myself, and they couldn't have either."[53]

The writing team of Miranda, Kitt, and Green worked on *Bring It On* for about two years before the show made its onstage debut—a short time for a musical that is likely Broadway-bound. The show premiered in Atlanta, Georgia, in January 2011 to mostly good reviews. However, after the run, it was clear to the creative team that revision and some recasting was needed. They took until late 2011 to cut songs and dialogue and write new material. Then, *Bring It On* started a national tour, opening in Los Angeles, California, on October 30, 2011. This was an unusual way to bring a musical to life, especially since the creative team hoped it would reach Broadway. More commonly, a show plays to Broadway audiences and then a national tour is launched.

Still, after more tweaking by the creative team, *Bring It On* made it to Broadway's St. James Theatre in previews July 12, 2012, and opened August 1, 2012.

Miranda found great personal growth working with the team on *Bring It On*. He learned new ways to write, too. Blankenbuehler, in his first foray into directing a show instead of just choreographing (though he did that, too), knew exactly what rhythms and tempos he wanted for certain songs. Miranda would write down the rhythm and beats per minute (BPM) and write a song based on it, essentially learning to work on the music backwards. The *Bring It On* experience also prepared him for writing for future productions. Both Miranda and Alex Lacamoire, who orchestrated *Bring It On*, have said they used too many prerecorded and electronic pieces in the score.

Used to writing on his own, Miranda also enjoyed the experience of having other songwriters to work with: "You don't get to go in the trenches with another songwriter unless you're the half of a Kander and Ebb … I got to be part of Miranda, Green, Kitt, and that was enormous fun … We sort of found a way to write the show that … really involved us all."[54]

Right Hand Men

When considering *Hamilton*, many focus solely on Miranda as the creator. However, as Oskar Eustis said on the Broadway Backstory podcast, "Part of Lin's genius is that he surrounds himself with people who bring out the best in him and the best in each other."[55]

The Cabinet

As he wrote what would become *Hamilton*, Miranda assembled a familiar team: Kail to direct, Blankenbuehler to choreograph, and Lacamoire as music director. All three had worked with him on *In the Heights*, and he collaborated with Lacamoire and Blankenbuehler on *Bring It On*. Miranda calls them "the Cabinet." To him, this team is an integral part of the creative process: "It's impossible to overstate it ... I bring a song in to them, and it's like a pit crew with a car. The song's going to come out leaner and faster as a result."[1]

1. Quoted in Suzy Evans, "The Cabinet Behind Lin-Manuel Miranda's 'Hamilton,'" *American Theatre*, August 6, 2015. www.americantheatre.org/2015/08/06/the-cabinet-behind-lin-manuel-mirandas-hamilton.

With the Cabinet (shown here from left: Blankenbuehler, Miranda, Lacamoire, and Kail), Miranda found a group that pushed him and each other to finish a project as well as make it better as they worked together.

When Miranda was reading Chernow's book, he told Kail about it. However, the White House performance video was the first time Kail had heard any music Miranda had written based on the book. Two years went by, however, and Miranda had only written two songs—the opening song "Alexander Hamilton" and "My Shot." Some of this was due to Miranda working on *West Side Story*, *Bring It On*, and other opportunities. Some of it was the difficulty of working on a brand new idea. Miranda told *Vogue* about the phases he goes through when starting to write something: "You go through the I'm a Fraud phase. You go through the I'll Never Finish phase. And every once in a while you think, What if I actually have created what I set out to create, and it's received as such?"[56]

A testament to the extraordinary relationship between composer and director, Kail finally stepped in after Miranda performed "My Shot" at a benefit in the summer of 2011. Miranda was still toying with the idea of *The Hamilton Mixtape*, but whatever the project would become, Kail gave Miranda the encouragement he needed to keep going with it. "The one thing I find really useful with this particular group is just planting some flags on the horizon so we can march toward them," Kail told *American Theatre* magazine. "And Lin responds very well to that, and once the

Miranda and John Kander met when Kander saw *In the Heights* on Broadway. Though more than 50 years apart in age, they started having lunch and talking about music.

flow state begins with him, it's really just about maintaining it."[57] One of the "flags" Kail planted for Miranda to reach was six months away at the *American Songbook* series at Lincoln Center in New York City in January 2012. With this performance on the horizon, Miranda wrote 10 new songs for *Hamilton* in those 6 months—a truly Hamilton-like pace. The performance took place on Alexander Hamilton's 255th birthday, and the audience was enthusiastic about the songs Miranda, a few actors—including Christopher Jackson—and a band led by Lacamoire presented. Miranda knew they had done well: "I saw John Kander's face light up during the rap battles between Hamilton and Jefferson … and I knew that we had something."[58]

In most shows, it is only after a score is completed that an orchestrator and music director like Lacamoire joins the team. Since that first time sharing "Alexander Hamilton," Miranda had been bringing Lacamoire music ideas for the piece ranging from just chords to complete demo recordings of new songs. "When he brings in a piece of music, he really gives me the freedom to explore stuff. He really allows me to put a stamp on it. I really get to play and suggest,"[59] Lacamoire said of working with Miranda. Miranda relishes this kind of collaboration: "Working with other people just makes you smarter, that's proven … And this is not a singular art form—it's 12 art forms smashed together. We elevate each other."[60]

The *American Songbook* performance would be the catalyst for the team known as the Cabinet to move forward in creating the show. After the presentation, Jeffrey Seller, who produced *In the Heights* as well as the famed original Broadway production of *Rent*, approached the team about taking the project to the next step: the stage.

Coming into Focus

It was finally clear to Miranda, as well as Kail, that *The Hamilton Mixtape* could be done as a musical theater work. Over the next year, they and Seller met to see what Miranda was writing and talk about the story of the show. There was a lot of writing to do—and simply writing does not pay the bills. Miranda was

Making His Name

The year 2012 proved that Miranda had become a star in the theater world as both a performer and a writer. First, he performed the role of Charlie Kringas in *Merrily We Roll Along* as part of the City Center Encores! production. He also contributed new songs to an Off-Broadway revival of the musical *Working*, which opened at the end of 2012.

offered a part on an NBC TV show called *Do No Harm* that filmed in Philadelphia, Pennsylvania, in late 2012. Miranda's character, Dr. Ruben Marcado, was not one of the top characters and would die in episode 11—so he took the job. "*Do No Harm* was like a writing residency for me,"[61] he told Grantland. He liked that it filmed so close to home and that he would be alone and able to write most days.

Then, *Bring It On* closed December 12, 2012, and Miranda was once again without a show on Broadway. Despite a short run, it was nominated for Best Musical at the Tony Awards and the writing team of Miranda and Green were nominated for a Drama Desk Award for Outstanding Lyrics in 2013.

Miranda was looking to the future: "I knew I had *Hamilton* in my pocket and I knew I needed to focus and time to get it done, and that was the hard part, because I have a family and I'm trying to support them."[62]

Chapter **Four**

"Blow Us All Away"

Over the course of 2012 and the beginning of 2013, the *Hamilton* project went through readings, and actors began becoming attached to the show. One of the early actors who would stay with the show was Phillipa Soo, playing the part of Hamilton's wife Elizabeth Schuyler. She told the Broadway Backstory podcast about her first experiences with the show: "There's something about it that in learning the music, you feel it in your heart, and you start to feel the impulse, and what are the actions behind it—which is the brilliance of Lin-Manuel Miranda."[63]

Hamilton *Summer Camp*

Miranda, Kail, and Lacamoire headed to Vassar College in upstate New York during the summer of 2013 to focus completely on *The Hamilton Mixtape* musical. Miranda had been invited to workshop the musical as part of the Powerhouse Theater season produced by the New York Stage and Film Company, a nonprofit theater company that gives artists time and space to develop new pieces of work. Miranda, Kail, and Lacamoire spent eight days living together and focusing only on the *Hamilton* project. The stay ended in two performances at which they presented the complete Act One of *The Hamilton Mixtape* with actors playing the roles, including Miranda as Hamilton. There were no sets or costumes, and only about 150 people saw each presentation. Like the *American Songbook* presentation, it was a very public showcase of a project that was still in the early stages—and there were no guarantees it would make it out of the workshop phase.

The "Hip-Hop Musical"

From the outset, Lin-Manuel Miranda knew the premise of *Hamilton* could be hard to sell: a musical about the life of lesser-known Founding Father Alexander Hamilton. What might be even harder for traditional theater-going audiences to swallow was a story largely told through rap and hip-hop. Miranda faced this obstacle when writing *In the Heights*. He told the Broadway Backstory podcast he had played it safe when including hip-hop in that show, using rap in bursts interrupted by a traditionally sung chorus when the audience might need a break. Producer Jeffery Seller suspected *In the Heights* alienated some audience members before they even saw the show: "If it didn't have that label of hip-hop painted on it all the time it would still be running, because it was a beautiful, emotionally satisfying show."[64]

Miranda did not want to limit himself in that way again. He believed deeply that not only was Hamilton's story a familiar hip-hop narrative, it would be best told with the genre. Hamilton wrote an enormous amount during his life, including letters, the Federalist Papers arguing for the ratification of the U.S. Constitution, and thousands of other pieces of writing. Miranda wanted to draw upon this body of work and impress upon the audience how much Hamilton had to say. It was also a way to fit in more of the story: "What hip-hop allows me to do is add more lyrics per capita than any other musical going. Its capacity to pack information in a way that is dense but still understandable is incredibly useful."[65]

The time Miranda spent writing *Hamilton*, as the show was now called, as *The Hamilton Mixtape* was not time wasted, in Miranda's opinion:

I wanted it to be as dense as my favorite hip-hop albums and my favorite musical albums, where I'm still catching allusions or alliteration or double meanings or triple entendres that I didn't catch the first time. I wouldn't have packed it this tight if I were writing for the stage—but by packing it that tight and never letting up on that, I think we've ended up with a much richer show.[66]

For a time, Miranda tried working with a playwright and using dialogue between songs, but after the fiery opening number, it was hard to go back to characters simply speaking to one another. Miranda found hip-hop to allow for conversational exchanges between characters as well; not everything had to be at a frantic pace or rapped with very heightened emotions. He was able to draw on his extensive knowledge of hip-hop and rap to make each song sound like it would have a place on a rap album instead of hip-hop written for theater. "There's been lots of theater that uses hip-hop in it, but more often than not it's used as a joke—isn't it hilarious that these characters are rapping … I treat it as a musical form,"[67] Miranda said.

Calling *Hamilton* a hip-hop musical would be doing the piece a disservice as it contains more than just hip-hop. From pop songs inspired by the Beatles to songs that sound like traditional Broadway ballads, *Hamilton* is a true mixture of all the music Miranda grew up listening to. Oskar Eustis told the *New York Times* that Miranda's deep love for both musical theater and hip-hop served him well in writing *Hamilton*: "His ability to work in both of those forms is inseparable from the fact that he loves both forms—he's not being a tourist when he visits one or the other, but he's deeply embedded in both of them."[68]

Public Partnership

In the fall of 2013, Miranda finally accepted Oskar Eustis's invitation to work on the *Hamilton* project at the Public Theater. Eustis said at that point, the story of the musical was not quite decided yet. There were songs in characters' voices, but it was not clear how those songs would fit together. The Public sponsored two

Easter Eggs

Hamilton is full of references to the world outside of itself, including rap, other theater shows, and history. In one of King George's songs, he references going mad, which King George did years later. There are references to songs by the Notorious B.I.G. as well as *The Last Five Years*, a musical by Jason Robert Brown. Even Burr's narration of the show was inspired by Andrew Lloyd Webber's musicals—in both *Evita* and *Jesus Christ Superstar*, the title character's nemesis narrates, just like Burr in *Hamilton*.

Miranda often gives credit to the theater creators who came before him, such as Andrew Lloyd Webber, when he is inspired by their work. Webber's choice of narrators in some of his shows inspired Miranda's decision to have Aaron Burr narrate *Hamilton*.

workshops for the show. After each one, Miranda, the creative team, and Eustis would talk about what was working and what was not. Songs were cut as these workshops went on, including a rap battle about slavery. Characters changed, and one was even cut—Benjamin Franklin. Miranda said Franklin and Hamilton did not interact enough to keep him, even though he liked the song Franklin would have sung.

A fully staged and costumed Act One and read-through of Act Two occurred in the spring of 2014. Andy Blankenbuehler added choreography, and set designer David Korins created some scenery for the performance. At this point, the Cabinet was working with a full company of actors as well. From the beginning, Miranda had been picturing musicians of the hip-hop world as the characters he was writing. This inspired the very first casting notices he had ever written, which included mash-ups of musical theater characters, music artists, and rappers to help potential cast members better understand what they were auditioning for:

AARON BURR … Javert [the adversary of Jean Valjean in Les Misérables] *meets Mos Def*

GEORGE WASHINGTON … John Legend meets Mufasa [the father in Disney's The Lion King]

HERCULES MULLIGAN … Busta Rhymes meets Donald O'Connor [a 1940s movie star best known for Singin' in the Rain]

MARIA REYNOLDS … [Jazmine] Sullivan meets Carla from Nine[69]

In writing these mash-ups as part of the character breakdown, Miranda wanted to cast a wider net for talent. He wanted to offer a point of entry for both musical theater performers by including a reference to musical characters, such as Carla from *Nine*, and hip-hop specialists by including artists such as Busta Rhymes.

Daveed Diggs, a rapper who would take on the roles of Marquis de Lafayette and Thomas Jefferson and make his Broadway debut in *Hamilton*, commented to *Rolling Stone* about how clear the voice of each character was—just like the casting notices seemed

to indicate: "When you're developing your voice as a rapper, you figure out your cadence—your swag—and that's how you write … Lin managed to figure that out for *all* of these different characters … And that's really impressive."[70]

The casting notice also noted that all ethnicities were being considered. For a musical about the founding of the United States by primarily white men, this was revolutionary. Miranda, who had already been envisioning the Founding Fathers with the diversity of the hip-hop landscape, credits Kail

Daveed Diggs knew Miranda from performing with Freestyle Love Supreme before starting to work on *Hamilton.*

with voicing the idea. However, Miranda said he always wanted the cast to be inclusive: "The idea has always been to look the way

The cast of *Hamilton* (shown here in 2016) includes white, black, and Latinx actors—and no part has a set ethnicity. Though Miranda is Puerto Rican, black actor Michael Luwoye took over the part of Alexander Hamilton in January 2018.

Emmy Winner

In 2013, Miranda teamed up with Tom Kitt again. They wrote a song called "Bigger" for the 67th Annual Tony Awards, which integrated nods to the shows on Broadway that season, including *Once*, *Kinky Boots*, and *Matilda*. Tony Awards host Neil Patrick Harris performed it with help from the casts of the nominated shows and Mike Tyson. The song won Miranda and Kitt the Emmy Award for Outstanding Original Music and Lyrics in 2014.

America looks now, and that doesn't exclude anyone."[71] Leslie Odom Jr., a black actor who was cast as Aaron Burr, confirmed that Miranda and Kail's intent was achieved: "It is quite literally taking the history that someone has tried to exclude us from and reclaiming it ... We are saying we have the right to tell it too."[72]

Wrestling with History

As *The Hamilton Mixtape* was evolving into *Hamilton* the musical, Miranda had to continually refocus on what the major arc of the story would be while still keeping it as historically accurate as possible. At the start, Kail and Miranda made lists of topics, people, and ideas from Chernow's book. Then, they compared lists to see what they both liked or were struck by. That was what Miranda focused on writing about. It was only one step in wrangling the life of Alexander Hamilton and the huge history of the early United States.

Miranda sought help from his friend John Weidman, the book writer of two history-centric musicals, *Assassins* and *Pacific Overtures*. Weidman advised Miranda that it would be impossible to include everything about that time period and Hamilton's life. Weidman said, "forgive yourself in advance for not getting it all

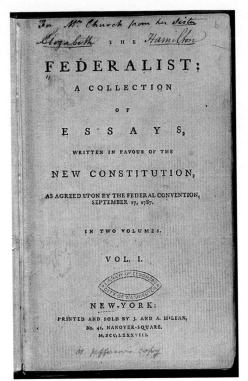

Beginning in 1955, Columbia University began collecting the letters, reports from government work, and other writings of Alexander Hamilton. Miranda had a lot to look to for inspiration for the show.

and start to dramatize the moments that make you think this thing sings."[73]

Miranda did need to alter history in some places to suit the stage as the story became clearer to him. For example, Hamilton's sister-in-law Angelica sings that her father, politician Philip Schuyler, has no sons. In reality, Philip Schuyler raised many children, including a son, not just three daughters as depicted in *Hamilton*. When Miranda made changes like this, he made sure they served the story: "Whenever I was in doubt as to creative license, I would always go back to his [Hamilton's] writings. That was the gut check. And if you start from the premise that the truth is more interesting, that created the contours of our show."[74] He knew that at its core, *Hamilton* was Alexander Hamilton's story, and he stuck to that idea carefully.

Miranda needed the numerous historical figures in *Hamilton*, from George Washington to James Madison, to ring true, too. He did not want to present them as they often are in classrooms, as one-dimensional models of virtue and patriotism: "I think our goal is to present them as human, and not just the five facts you know about them from our history books."[75] He wanted to show that "they had fights and they compromised and they did their best to hold this fragile thing together. They were making it up as they went along and so are we."[76]

Though more work would be done honing the show as workshops progressed, the lucky few who saw the early workshops of *Hamilton* already thought Miranda had gotten all of it right—the history, the casting, and the tone. Acclaimed playwright John Guare went to one of the workshops at the Public with a friend and gave a glowing review: "I haven't felt this alive in a show since I don't know when ... He had captured the spirit of Hamilton, and the spirit of Ron Chernow's book, and the spirit of the time."[77]

Two Beginnings

Following the two workshops at the Public, *Hamilton* was set to take the stage as an Off-Broadway production in previews January 2015 and officially open February 17, 2015. Miranda and the rest of the creative team were hard at work putting the show on its feet. Chernow recalls Miranda checking in with him at this time, emailing him songs as they worked toward the Off-Broadway opening. Eustis told *American Theatre* about seeing Miranda rework the song "Washington on Your Side": "It's just beautiful to watch him figure out how to take a beautiful thing and then activate it so it unleashes its full dramatic potential. That's the kind of brain he has; it's thrilling to be around."[78]

While Miranda was knee-deep in completing *Hamilton* and preparing to perform in it, he was preparing for another role: father. His wife was pregnant with their first child during the break between the final Public workshop and the opening of the Off-Broadway run. Sebastian Miranda was born November 10, 2014, just two weeks before Lin-Manuel Miranda began rehearsals for *Hamilton* Off-Broadway. Miranda praised his wife for dealing with the difficult timing: "She's the superhero in all of this because she had to deal with a newborn kid during tech."[79]

Sebastian's birth may have helped Miranda finally finish part of *Hamilton*'s ending. He had long been struggling with how to put Hamilton's death by duel on stage: "What was going on in Hamilton's head in those final moments? ... I am going

@Lin_Manuel

When the *New Yorker* article, "All About the Hamiltons" came out February 9, 2015, it chronicled the making of *Hamilton*, gave insight to its writing, and introduced the primary creative characters of the venture. However, anyone who followed Miranda on Twitter @Lin_Manuel already knew of many moments and breakthroughs in *Hamilton*'s writing from the beginning of the idea. Miranda told *American Theatre* that Twitter became a "substitute for caffeine on all my writing jags."[1]

1. Quoted in Suzy Evans, "How 'Hamilton' Found Its Groove," *American Theatre*, July 27, 2015. www.americantheatre.org/2015/07/27/how-hamilton-found-its-groove/.

to be making that guess until Tommy forces me to put my pen down."[80] Then, on the morning of New Year's Day 2015, it came to him. Miranda was in bed, with Sebastian sleeping on him, and his wife, Vanessa, sleeping next to him. It was profoundly quiet—and he realized that was the one thing he had not yet done in *Hamilton*. So, he went out to walk the dog with just a notebook and started writing the only part of the show with no music under it, Alexander Hamilton's last moments alive, inspired by new moments of life.

The quiet of Miranda's domestic life must have seemed even quieter in comparison to the building buzz around *Hamilton*. The first preview, which at the Public was ticketed for free by lottery using a ticketing app, garnered about 12,000 entries. The usual amount of entries for other shows was about 1,000. Additionally, the show's whole run was sold out before it even opened. Still, it was tough for Miranda and the rest of the creative team to predict what the Off-Broadway opening would bring.

Becoming Hamilton

When *Hamilton* opened Off-Broadway, Miranda said, "It's sad to say goodbye to writing it, but it's such a joy to say hello to getting to be in it every night with this incredible company."[81] It was time to own another aspect of the creation of *Hamilton*: taking on its title role.

At no point in the many years of presenting the different stages of *Hamilton* had any else played Alexander Hamilton but Miranda himself. For a time, though, Miranda contemplated playing Aaron Burr, the narrator and man who eventually shoots Hamilton in a duel. He recognized Burr in himself, in the feelings he had in his life when friends had gotten success before him: "I feel very Burr-like when I think what Hamilton accomplished by that age [35]. Or Paul McCartney. Or Sondheim. Or Gershwin. Or OutKast. My jaw drops in awe of that kind of work ethic."[82] However, when the creative team found Leslie Odom Jr., Miranda knew Odom was the sound of Burr and no one else should play the character.

Miranda also saw himself in the Hamilton character. They both wrote a lot, for one thing: "What I share with Hamilton … is that I want to get as many of the ideas out of my head as possible in the time I have."[83] This was recognized as Hamiltonian by Phillipa Soo, too: "I remember him coming into the rehearsal room in his slippers, because he'd been across the street writing. And I was like, 'Oh, my God, this guy is nonstop!' Kind of like Hamilton."[84] Tommy Kail also saw the parallels between Hamilton and Miranda: "This idea of Hamilton being so conscious of a ticking clock is very much a match for Lin's biochemistry."[85] That was an aspect of Hamilton Miranda also noticed within himself: "When I wrote Hamilton's lyric 'I imagine death so much it feels more like a memory,' I was like, 'O.K., I know this guy.'"[86] On the other hand, Miranda also relished the freedom of playing Hamilton. He liked being cocky, super smart, and a bit more reckless than he would be in everyday life.

Miranda really fell into the role of Usnavi in *In the Heights*. His choice to perform as Hamilton was much more intentional. Having had the experience of the grueling eight shows a week

Hamilton depicts Alexander Hamilton's life from about age 19 to his death in his late 40s. Changes to the character's clothing, wig, and glasses helped Miranda convincingly portray such a big age range.

of the Broadway run, Miranda knew he could handle it. Besides, though he played the title character, he did not feel the whole show was on his shoulders: "For me, the show's the star; I'm not the star. It really is this ensemble piece."[87]

It's a Hit!

Hamilton opened to rave reviews Off-Broadway at the Public. Ben Brantley, theater critic for the *New York Times*, wrote that it was the first musical in decades to accurately incorporate music of the time. Brantley nearly gushed about Miranda as a writer and performer: "The sheer scope of what Mr. Miranda crams into his precisely but exuberantly chiseled lyrics is a marvel ... Ambitious, enthusiastic and talented in equal measures, Mr. Miranda embodies those sentiments [young, scrappy, and hungry] in a show that aims impossibly high and hits its target."[88]

The run of the show at the Public was extended three times, allowing *Hamilton*'s buzz to build to a roar. From Dick Cheney to Madonna, celebrities of all kinds began to fill the seats at

When rapper Nas came to see *Hamilton*, Miranda was so starstruck, he gave Nas his original copy of Chernow's book.

the Public. Michelle Obama, then the First Lady, saw the show Off-Broadway and told Oskar Eustis privately afterward that it was "the greatest work of art I have ever seen in any medium,"[89] a sentiment she would repeat later on the record.

Already, the community that had mostly missed *In the Heights* was recognizing Miranda's hip-hop prowess. Busta Rhymes, Questlove, and RZA, all hip-hop heroes of Miranda's, came to see *Hamilton* at the Public, and they loved it. Miranda later told *Rolling Stone* that his "secret dream"[90] was that hip-hop artists would embrace *Hamilton*, and he felt like his dream had come true. That did not make it any less nerve-wracking to know his heroes were in the audience. On the night Busta Rhymes came to the show, Miranda said he had to remind himself not to look at him: "It was just … crazy, when the people you've emptied your pockets to see are seeing you … It's both ennobling and totally humbling and totally terrifying. But after Busta, everything was cool."[91]

Waiting for Its Broadway Debut

At the 2015 Drama Desk Awards, Miranda won awards for Outstanding Music, Outstanding Lyrics, and Outstanding Book of a Musical—three of the seven awards *Hamilton* took home that night. Miranda won a Lucille Lortel Award for Outstanding Lead Actor in a Musical for the Off-Broadway performance. He was also awarded a 2015 Obie Award for Best New American Theatre Work for *Hamilton* and Outer Critic Circle Awards for Outstanding Book of a Musical and Outstanding New Score.

It was no surprise when a Broadway transfer was announced. However, the opening date did surprise some people. Because of *Hamilton*'s Off-Broadway success, the cast and crew could have moved the show to Broadway almost immediately after closing at the Public. That would make them the last Broadway show to open in the 2015 season to be eligible for the Tony Awards. Miranda and Kail decided not to do that, for two main reasons.

First, considering the show's awards already, it seemed likely to do well at the Tony Awards. Miranda and his team did not want to block the recognition of other innovative new musicals that came out that season, particularly *Fun Home* and *An American in Paris*. Eustis said Miranda did not want to be the "bully" on Broadway and wanted to allow Jeanine Tesori, the composer of *Fun Home*, to win a Tony: "That kind of consciousness is just so Lin. He's so beautiful that way."[92]

It was easy for the *Hamilton* team be generous to other theater artists because they had a second major reason for waiting to open on Broadway. Both Miranda and Kail wanted to make some changes to the show before it reached Broadway. Miranda rewrote Hamilton's final soliloquy after the closing of *Hamilton* at the Public on May 3, 2015. He also reworked a song called "One Last Ride" that was about the Whiskey Rebellion to "One Last Time" about Washington stepping down from office. "The Schuyler Sisters" also received a makeover as Alex Lacamoire worked on new orchestrations and vocal lines based on the talented women playing the three sisters. All of these alterations were to make the show the best it could be.

Still, the turnaround time was tight. The creative team and cast had only 70 days to write and implement these and other changes, as well as complete sets for the new space. Miranda told *Vogue* that recognizing what changes needed to be made was difficult, like a "lobster trying to give notes from inside the pot."[93]

On Broadway

Hamilton would become the first Broadway show to open in the 2016 Tony Awards season. It was able to open in the same theater *In the Heights* played in for three years, the Richard Rodgers Theatre. When he announced this to the cast, Miranda told them—many of whom had been part of *In the Heights*—that they were going "home."[94]

By the time *Hamilton* was in opening previews on July 13, 2015, the show had sold almost 200,000 advance tickets, which was more than $27 million. While impressive, this number did not include the in-person lottery for $10 front-row seats that was held every performance at the Richard Rodgers. The night of the first preview, 704 people came to try their luck at winning these few tickets. Miranda, who was in the theater when he heard so many had shown up to try and see the show, did not want those who did not win to walk away with nothing. Eustis, who was with him at the time, said Miranda grabbed a megaphone and walked out to the crowd and said: "So, thanks to you, we're probably going to be here a while, so don't be disappointed if you don't win today. I love you very much. Yay Hamlet!"[95] (Miranda made a *Hamlet* reference because a woman previously drove by him congratulating him on writing William Shakespeare's *Hamlet*, not *Hamilton*.)

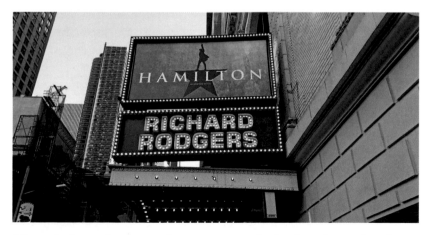

Miranda kept the same dressing room he had in the Richard Rodgers Theatre for *In the Heights* for his run in *Hamilton*.

Hundreds of people came to see Ham4Ham before every performance at the Richard Rodgers Theatre. The tradition continued as *Hamilton* began to be performed in other cities as well.

This crowd interaction before each performance while audience members waited for lottery winners to be announced became routine. They called it Ham4Ham. Over time, other *Hamilton* cast members, Broadway stars, and celebrities, including Mandy Gonzales and Patti LuPone, would come with Miranda to talk to the crowd and perform before each show. YouTube videos of the various goofy performances would get thousands of views, and attendees started using #Ham4Ham when sharing video clips and photos from the event. Even more buzz built around *Hamilton* as Ham4Ham became popular in and of itself. Miranda turned a genuine wish to connect with fans into a viral phenomenon.

On August 6, 2015, *Hamilton* officially opened at the Richard Rodgers Theatre. On the red carpet before the show, Miranda told reporters that it was the culmination of seven years of hard work: "This has been the finish line for such a long time. And you know, we have a show tomorrow night. So, that will keep me humble."[96] The glowing reviews the show received could have challenged that humility, but that is not Miranda, on or off the stage. As the *Washington Post*'s review noted, "Miranda's own performance feels weighty without being showy; it's generous to his sparkling castmates."[97]

Genius?

When others talk about Miranda, if they do not use the word "genius" to describe him, they often come close. Ron Chernow told *Smithsonian* he was not sure if Miranda was a genius: "Hamilton was a genius ... But Lin's made a masterpiece."[98] Oskar Eustis compared Miranda to one of the greatest writers for theater of all time: "I think Lin's ambitions are Shakespearean, and I think his achievement is Shakespearean ... And I run the New York Shakespeare Festival!"[99]

As is typical of Miranda, he shrugs the moniker off: "I'm not a ... genius. I work my [butt] off. Hamilton could have written what I wrote in about three weeks. *That's* genius."[100] His father tends to agree, highlighting what he sees as one of his son's best qualities instead: "A genius? I'm not sure what that word means ... What I admire most about [Lin] is his humility."[101]

In September 2015, Miranda earned the title of "genius" honestly, by receiving a fellowship from the MacArthur Foundation, often called a "genius grant." Miranda was one of twenty-four people awarded the honor, a group that included scientists, writers, and scholars in history and economics. Each recipient receives $625,000 over 5 years. The MacArthur Foundation wrote of Miranda on their website: "Melding a love of the musical with a pop culture sensibility, Miranda is expanding the conventions of mainstream theater and showcasing the cultural riches of the American urban panorama."[102]

Back to the Music

In September 2015, the original Broadway cast recording of *Hamilton* was released digitally. It earned its hip-hop bona fides before it even came out, having been produced by two hip-hop legends: Questlove and Black Thought of the Roots. It had the largest first week sales for a digital cast album ever and debuted at number 12 on the Billboard chart when the physical album came out in October. Perhaps more impressive, the album hit number 1 on the Billboard Rap Charts during the week of November 28. Miranda's dream of being accepted by the rap community was coming true in a big way.

Soon after, *Hamilton* was nominated for the Best Musical Theater Album Grammy Award. Even more exciting was the invitation for Miranda and the cast of the show to perform on the Grammys, an infrequent occurrence for musicals. They performed the opening number, "Alexander Hamilton," from the stage of the Richard Rodgers Theatre. That was where Miranda gave his acceptance speech when the album won, too. Miranda once again gave his thank you speech in rap form:

> We write music, we write songs to tell a story,
>
> whether you're King Kendrick or Jeanine Tesori.
>
> I'm sorry if I start screaming these thanks hysterically,
>
> John Buzzetti, Tim Latham, Tom Coyne, and Derek Lee,
>
> Tommy Kail set the stage to kick our boots through.
>
> Bill Sherman, Quest, and Tariq, the whole Roots crew;
>
> Sean at Warner Chapel, Riggs and Craig at Atlantic;
>
> Lacamoire, my right-hand man, this frantic Hispanic
>
> is non-stop. The best idea goes in the pot
>
> whether you're Harnick and Bock, Pun, Biggie, or Pac.
>
> The cast, unstoppable, band is unbeatable,
>
> inimitable, inevitable, always inspiring me to pull through.
>
> Vanessa, Angie, Illie, Ellie, we adore you.
>
> Sebastian, Daddy's bringing home a Grammy for you.
>
> Good night![103]

Music service Spotify reported that the cast recording of *Hamilton* had been streamed almost half a billion times during 2016. By August 2017, the album had sold more than 1.285 million copies and spent more than 100 weeks on the Billboard charts.

Awards Season

Miranda was nominated for the prestigious Pulitzer Prize for Drama for *In the Heights* in 2009. In 2016, he was nominated again for *Hamilton*. In April 2016, it was announced that he won, making *Hamilton* only the ninth musical to ever win the yearly prize. Miranda released a statement reacting to the win, quoting his own show: "To win today for *Hamilton* is beyond my wildest dreams … Look at where we are. Look at where we started."[104]

Miranda was not done being honored yet. On May 3, 2016, he sat at home with his parents and *In the Heights* book writer Quiara Alegría Hudes and screamed every time *Hamilton* was nominated for another Tony Award. In the end, the show would be nominated for 16 Tony Awards, setting a new record for the most nominations in the history of the award show. Miranda was nominated in three categories himself: Best Book of a Musical, Best Original Score, and Best Performance by an Actor in a Leading Role in a Musical. As a nominee for Best Musical, the cast of *Hamilton* was set to perform at the June 12, 2016, show.

Tony Awards Day

The morning of June 12, Miranda headed to the theater around 7 a.m. to rehearse the Tony Awards opening number and "Yorktown (The World Turned Upside Down)," which the cast would perform in full costume and with full choreography. Around 1 p.m., he got some terrible news.

Early that morning, a shooting at Pulse nightclub in Orlando, Florida, had become the worst mass shooting in the United States up to that point. The attack hit Miranda hard as the club was hosting its weekly Latin night, and it was a gay nightclub, a demographic known to be a big part of the theater community.

However, the Tony Awards would go on, beginning with a short tribute delivered by host James Corden. Miranda wanted to show solidarity and support, too. The creative team behind *Hamilton* decided to perform their number, which was depicting battle, without the prop guns used in the show.

Hamilton would go on to win 11 awards, the second-most wins of any show ever. Partly due to *Hamilton* and Miranda's bold casting choices, for the first time in history, a person of color won every acting category, too. When Leslie Odom Jr. won for Best Performance by an Actor in a Leading Role in a Musical for his portrayal of Aaron Burr, he addressed Miranda: "Lin-Manuel, God bless you man, really. You've given us a new vision of what's possible."[105]

Miranda went on to win both Best Book of a Musical and Best Score. When he received his award for Best Score, he told the Tony Awards crowd, "I'm not freestyling. I'm too old. I wrote you a sonnet instead," and gave his acceptance speech in poem form:

My wife's the reason anything gets done

She nudges me towards promise by degrees.

She is a perfect symphony of one,

Our son is her most beautiful reprise.

We chase the melodies that seem to find us

Until they're finished songs and start to play.

When senseless acts of tragedy remind us

That nothing here is promised, not one day.

This show is proof that history remembers.

We live through times when hate and fear seem stronger.

We rise and fall and light from dying embers,

Amid national tragedy, Miranda was able to say what people were possibly feeling as well as offer hope for the future in his acceptance speech at the 2016 Tony Awards.

Remembrances that hope and love lasts longer.

And love is love is love is love is love is love is love is love is love,

Cannot be killed or swept aside,

I sing Vanessa's symphony, Eliza tells her story,

Now fill the world with music love and pride.[106]

He used the phrase "love is love" as a tribute to the LGBT+ community that was targeted by the shooting in Orlando. He later said he wanted to keep saying it like an "incantation:" "When you write musicals, you're trying to meet the moment honestly, and I felt like I had a duty to meet the moment as honestly as I could with what I had in me."[107]

Chapter **Five**

How Far
He Will Go

On March 14, 2016, Lin-Manuel Miranda's journey with *Hamilton* came full circle. He returned to the White House to perform parts of the show, this time with the cast and more than 16 bars to show off. First Lady Michelle Obama continued to champion the show using that special word Miranda so often shrugs off: "We knew that this had the potential to be really, really good based on his performance, but what we didn't know and never could have imagined [was] that it would be a work of genius. True genius."[108] Still, even with praise from the First Lady at the White House, *Hamilton*'s—and Miranda's—reach was only just beginning.

One Last Time

Miranda performed his last show as the full-time Alexander Hamilton in the Broadway production of *Hamilton* on July 9, 2016. When the news broke, Miranda was reported as saying that did not mean he would be done with the part forever: "This is a role I am going to be going back to again and again. I plan to revisit this role a lot."[109] Nonetheless, he told *GQ* he was ready to leave the role behind because he was beginning to feel like his family life and other pursuits were not being attended

While at the White House in 2016, Miranda performed with the *Hamilton* cast and did a freestyle rap with President Obama in the Rose Garden.

to since he had to be ready and onstage at 8 p.m. every night: "Performing *Hamilton* through two hours and 45 minutes, when you're in it, was the most relaxing part of the day. Because I didn't have unanswered e-mails, or family stuff I wasn't doing. I was just supposed to be Hamilton, and I know the script on that one."[110]

During his run of *Hamilton*, Miranda achieved a level of fame that made him a household name, including being recognized when he would ride the subway around New York City. Near the end of Miranda's run in *Hamilton*, this level of recognition became unsafe. In the past, he would be able to leave by the stage door with the rest of the cast to say hello to fans, take pictures, and give autographs. However, so many people started coming to the stage door, he worried about kids near the barriers around the door getting crushed by the crowd. People who sold autographs online started becoming more aggressive in asking him for signatures. Fans were increasingly insistent in their need for selfies and autographs. So, for the last month Miranda was in the show, he had to leave the theater a secret way.

The Hamilton Mixtape, *Revisited*

In December 2016, Miranda's original vision of a concept album based on the life of Alexander Hamilton was realized. Following the release of the cast album, he tweeted that work was beginning in earnest on *The Hamilton Mixtape*. Questlove and Black Thought would again help produce the album, which, over the ensuing months, was revealed to be a mix of covers of songs from the show and remixes or interpretations of themes and music from *Hamilton*. When it was finished, *The Hamilton Mixtape* featured some of the biggest names in R&B and hip-hop, including Usher singing a faithful cover of "Wait For It;" a track using the chorus from "My Shot" and featuring rappers Busta Rhymes, Joell Ortiz, and Nate Ruess; and Chance the Rapper contributing to "Dear Theodosia (Reprise)." Pop superstars Kelly Clarkson, Alicia Keys, and Sia all contributed covers, too.

The mixtape offered a glimpse of what songs did not make it to the final version of *Hamilton*. On "Congratulations" singer Dessa takes the part of Angelica Schuyler, come to scold

In December 2016, a live Ham4Ham event at the Richard Rodgers Theatre featured artists from the mixtape—including Ashanti, Ja Rule, Regina Spektor, and Black Thought—performing their songs.

Hamilton for how he has treated his wife. Miranda included a demo of him singing a song called "Valley Forge" about the Continental Army's stay at Valley Forge during the winter of 1777 and 1778. He told *Entertainment Weekly* the song did not end up working in the show: "That was a demo I was always really proud of … but it isn't dramatically interesting to watch a bunch of people freezing to death slowly. I took the best lines from it and put them in a different song called 'Stay Alive.'"[111] A third "Cabinet Battle" song about slavery, a track that did not make it into the show either, is also featured on the mixtape. Miranda said he spent months writing the battle, but ultimately, since the Founding Fathers did not address the slavery question, it did not do much for the plot. However, Miranda was glad to include it on the mixtape: "It was worthy for me to write, and cathartic for me to write."[112]

The Hamilton Mixtape debuted at number 1 on the Billboard Hot 200 chart in December 2016. Since then, Miranda has spoken about creating a second volume to follow up the successful album. In December 2017, Miranda announced that he would release a Hamilton-related song every month until

December 2018 in a series he called "Hamildrops." The first was a song by the rock band the Decemberists called "Ben Franklin's Song." The track used lyrics Miranda had written for Benjamin Franklin that had been cut from the show.

Part of the Disney Family

Though *Hamilton*'s development demanded much of his time, Miranda spent three years working on another huge project at the same time: music for the Disney movie *Moana*. As he later told the *Hollywood Reporter* about the time he was working on both, "There's an adage if you want something done ask a busy person to do it because they're already in motion. That's basically how it felt. On the one hand, [*Moana*] provided an oasis in the general hecticness of my life in the *Hamilton* era and, on the other hand, I thrive under deadline."[113] Nonetheless, it was another dream job for Miranda, who was working with the directors of his favorite Disney animated movie, *The Little Mermaid*. *Moana* was not Miranda's first time writing for a Disney project. In 2015, he met director J. J. Abrams and ended up writing a scene of music for the cantina in *Star Wars: The Force Awakens*.

Miranda collaborated with Polynesian composer Opetaia Foa'i on the music for *Moana* to make sure he kept the rhythms and sounds of the movie authentic to the Pacific Islands where it took place. The task was a familiar one to Miranda:

You always want the people, the culture you're writing

Not only did Miranda write music for *Moana*, he also sings on the soundtrack in a song called "We Know the Way."

about, to be able to see themselves in the thing. I felt the same way when I was writing In The Heights. *I was representing my neighborhood and a lot of Caribbean rhythms. It wasn't just one island. It was Dominican and Puerto Rican and Cuban and Mexican and Latin American, and how do I write a score that reflects all that and has its own voice?*[114]

The longing of the main character, a teenage girl named Moana, was also familiar to Miranda. He tapped into his youthful dream to be an artist when writing "How Far I'll Go," the song that expresses Moana's feeling about her home and hopes for the future: "I realized it's not a song about a young woman who hates where she is and needs to get out, it's a song about a woman who loves where she lives and her family and her culture and still has this feeling."[115]

After the movie was released in November 2016, the song would go on to earn Miranda his first Oscar nomination. He took his mom to the ceremony because of a prediction she made when he was young: "I remember my mom—as a kid—saying, 'When you get nominated for an Oscar, I'm your date.' That's such a pie-in-the-sky thing to say. But she sort of always believed, I think she believed even before I did, so I'm thrilled to get to keep that promise."[116]

In the spring of 2016, another Disney project involving Miranda was announced. He would play a leading role in the sequel to *Mary Poppins*, *Mary Poppins Returns*, as a lamplighter named Jack. The part was first presented to Miranda while he was in *Hamilton*. In fact, he told *Entertainment Weekly* that he found out about it between a matinee and evening performance of the show. Choosing *Mary Poppins Returns* as his first foray into acting in a big movie was easy after he read the script and met with director Rob Marshall, who directed the movie version of the musical *Chicago*: "Rob made *Chicago*—I think it's the best modern musical adaptation we have—so I knew I wanted to be in that room and go on that ride … It's just this sort of iconic thing that's from your childhood, and it's crazy to even get to do it."[117] In addition to getting to

The Small Screen

Though he is new to big acting parts in movies, Miranda has been on a lot of TV shows. From a small part in *The Sopranos* as a bellman to spots on *Modern Family*, *Sesame Street*, and *How I Met Your Mother*, Miranda has appeared as characters as well as himself. In a 2017 episode of *Curb Your Enthusiasm*, he played himself being pitched a musical by the show's star, Larry David.

film in London and work with Marshall, Miranda was excited because he got to meet and work with theater and movie legend Dick Van Dyke.

"Love Make the World Go Round"

Miranda has said he has no interest in going into politics like his father, but he speaks out when he feels passionately about something. He often uses Twitter and other social media to do so, and he thinks carefully about what he wants to post: "I can't control the world, but I can control what I put into the world, so I try to have my timeline be a pretty bright spot for folks who may be fighting great fights elsewhere."[118] Sometimes, he uses music to spread a message. Not long after the shooting at Pulse nightclub in Orlando, Florida, in 2016, Miranda joined Jennifer Lopez on a song in tribute to the victims of the shooting called "Love Make the World Go Round." The money made from the song was donated to a program dedicated to a bilingual mental health program put on by the Hispanic Federation.

In 2017, Miranda released another song, "Almost Like Praying," raising money for a cause close to his heart: Puerto Rico. In September, the island was hit by Hurricane Maria, a terrible storm that caused flash floods, a loss of power for more

Miranda and Jennifer Lopez are shown here performing "Love Make the World Go Round" in New York City in July 2016.

than 3 million people, and as many as 1,000 deaths. Following the storm, relief efforts were greatly needed. Miranda wrote about the needs of those devastated by the storm in Puerto Rico, including family living there, in the *Hollywood Reporter*: "Puerto Ricans need supplies and resources just as badly as their fellow Americans in Texas and Florida, and this need is magnified by their geographic isolation from the mainland."[119]

Miranda conceived of a song using parts of the song "Maria" from *West Side Story* and a sung list of the 78 towns in Puerto Rico. He invited other Latinx singers and artists, including Marc Anthony, Jennifer Lopez, and Gloria Estefan, to record the names of the towns and other vocals on the song. It was released October 6, 2017, and came in at number 1 on the Billboard Digital Song Sales chart. It was downloaded more than 100,000 times, and Miranda said all the profits, which totaled more than $100,000, would go to relief in Puerto Rico. He also gave many interviews and attended the Tidal X benefit concert in Brooklyn, New York, which raised money for natural disaster relief efforts, including Hurricane Maria, to continue raising awareness about the issues facing Puerto Rico. He even put other projects on pause while speaking out about the

On November 19, 2017, Miranda spoke at a Unity for Puerto Rico rally held at the Lincoln Memorial in Washington, D.C., again showing his support for his family and friends in Puerto Rico.

damage on the island. Even months afterward, Miranda continued to remind the public that Puerto Rico needed funds, supplies, and support.

What Is a Legacy?

By the end of 2017, Miranda had been recognized for his contributions to the arts and the Latinx community and also received another Grammy nomination for "How Far I'll Go." In May 2017, Miranda, Kail, and a group of others awarded a young woman named Audrey Pratt the very first Wesleyan University *Hamilton* Prize for Creativity. The prize, named in honor of Miranda and Kail's achievement with *Hamilton*, gives a student a full scholarship to the university. Miranda and his family were awarded the President's Award at the Imagen Awards for their work in the arts and Latinx community. In early November 2017, it was announced that Miranda would receive the President's Merit Award at the Latin Grammys. This special award honors someone who has contributed to the betterment of the Latin community. It is not given every year, so when it is given out, it is a rare achievement.

At the Imagen Awards, Miranda said he was happy to see so many Latinx people making art, but he also said he would always like to see more.

These honors, added to Miranda's past successes and awards, are a testament to the legacy Miranda is building as both an artist and a Latino person in the spotlight. A theme Miranda has explored in his work, most particularly in *Hamilton*, legacy might be as important to Miranda as it had been to Alexander Hamilton. He has said he wants *Hamilton* to be in the league of *Fiddler on the Roof* and *West Side Story* as a musical that schools across the country are doing. However, he knows he cannot control how his work is seen years from now. He can only control how the work is made: "There will be times when 'Hamilton' is hailed. There will be times when 'Hamilton' is pilloried [publicly criticized] … The wind will do with it as it does. All you can do is throw the kite in the air."[120]

Even knowing that, Miranda still hears a ticking clock in his head. He spoke about people having two clocks in their head during his commencement address at Wesleyan in 2015. One clock is the super fast ticking many hear every day: "The other clock is in the distance, but it's slower and it's booming: that's the sound of the rest of your life, and what you're going to do with it in the time you have on this earth."[121] As Miranda has often said, this sound has been driving him all his life as he writes, perhaps like he is running out of time.

What Comes Next

Miranda continues to be nonstop in his work, but in 2018, his personal life caught up with his professional life again as he and his wife welcomed their second child, Francisco, on February 2.

Miranda has said he has other interests he would like to pursue outside of musical theater, but writing a book is not one of them: "I like the quiet it takes to pursue an idea the way I pursued *Hamilton*, but I couldn't write a book ... Because there's no applause at the end of writing a book."[122] He has worked hard to get better at writing for the stage, and he does not want to set that aside. However, he believes he can always improve his skills:

Miranda has plans to finally bring *Hamilton* to Puerto Rico—and star in it—in early 2019.

LeBron James goes and works on whatever he's weakest at in the off season, and that's what I'm going to go do. Hamilton *will be up, and I'll go work with songwriters I really love. One of the benefits of these hip-hop artists who come to the show who I really revere— like, I'll go sit in a studio and see how they write. Or I'll go maybe work on a screenplay or something. I just want to get better at the things I don't know. That's the goal.*[123]

Miranda is constantly on the lookout for a great idea, even while he continues working in TV and movies and raising awareness for the needs of the Latinx community, especially in Puerto Rico. He knows an idea will come to him. He just has to wait for it: "Your job as an artist is to chase your inspiration wherever it leads you. So, I'm waiting to fall in love again, then that'll be my next show."[124]

Notes

Introduction: Bursting onto Broadway

1. Quoted in Jesse David Fox, "In the Room Where It Happens, Eight Shows a Week," Vulture, January 11, 2016. www.vulture.com/2016/01/roundtable-interview-with-the-cast-of-hamilton.html.

2. Quoted in Michael Paulson, "Lin-Manuel Miranda, Creator and Star of 'Hamilton,' Grew Up on Hip-Hop and Show Tunes," *New York Times*, August 12, 2015. www.nytimes.com/2015/08/16/theater/lin-manuel-miranda-creator-and-star-of-hamilton-grew-up-on-hip-hop-and-show-tunes.html.

Chapter One: Creative Beginnings

3. Quoted in Rebecca Rubin, "Lin-Manuel Miranda and Family Celebrate Latino Community at Imagen Awards," *Variety*, August 9, 2017. variety.com/2017/scene/vpage/imagen-awards-lin-manuel-family-miranda-hamilton-latino-community-1202533598/.

4. Quoted in Rebecca Mead, "All About the Hamiltons," *New Yorker*, February 9, 2015. www.newyorker.com/magazine/2015/02/09/hamiltons.

5. Quoted in Fresh Air Podcast, "Lin-Manuel Miranda on Disney, Mixtapes and Why He Won't Try to Top 'Hamilton,'" NPR, January 3, 2017. www.npr.org/2017/01/03/507470975/lin-manuel-miranda-on-disney-mixtapes-and-why-he-wont-try-to-top-hamilton.

6. Quoted in Paulson, "Lin-Manuel Miranda, Creator and Star."

7. Quoted in Luchina Fisher, "5 Things to Know About 'Hamilton' Star Lin-Manuel Miranda," ABC News, May 3, 2016. abcnews.go.com/Entertainment/things-hamiltons-lin-manuel-miranda/story?id=38842029.

8. Quoted in Mead, "All About the Hamiltons."

9. Quoted in Fresh Air Podcast, "Lin-Manuel Miranda on Disney."

10. Quoted in Mark Binelli, "'Hamilton' Creator Lin-Manuel Miranda: The Rolling Stone Interview," *Rolling Stone*, June 1, 2016. www.rollingstone.com/music/features/hamilton-creator-lin-manuel-miranda-the-rolling-stone-interview-20160601.

11. Lin-Manuel Miranda, "Pursuing the Muse Against the Clock," *New York Times*, June 19, 2014. www.nytimes.com/2014/06/22/theater/lin-manuel-miranda-pays-tribute-to-jonathan-larson.html.

12. "Lin-Manuel Miranda in Conversation with Chris Jones," YouTube video, 1:08:43, posted by the Chicago Humanities Festival, September 28, 2016. www.youtube.com/watch?v=yDacl3CBx2M.

13. Miranda, "Pursuing the Muse."

14. Quoted in Fresh Air Podcast, "Lin-Manuel Miranda on Disney"

15. Quoted in Rembert Browne, "Genius: A Conversation with 'Hamilton' Maestro Lin-Manuel Miranda," Grantland, September 29, 2015. grantland.com/hollywood-prospectus/genius-a-conversation-with-hamilton-maestro-lin-manuel-miranda/.

16. Quoted in Browne, "Genius."

17. Quoted in Mead, "All About the Hamiltons."

18. Quoted in Binelli, "'Hamilton' Creator Lin-Manuel Miranda."

19. Quoted in Mead, "All About the Hamiltons."

Chapter Two: Reaching New Heights

20. Quoted in Mead, "All About the Hamiltons."

21. Quoted in Mead, "All About the Hamiltons."

22. "In the Heights: Chasing Broadway Dreams," 54:00, PBS "Great Performances," aired November 10, 2017. www.pbs.org/wnet/gperf/heights-chasing-broadway-dreams-full-episode/7642/?button=fullepisode.

23. "Lin-Manuel Miranda in Conversation with Chris Jones," YouTube video.

24. "In the Heights: Chasing Broadway Dreams," PBS "Great Performances."

25. Quoted in Browne, "Genius."

26. "In the Heights: Chasing Broadway Dreams," PBS "Great Performances."

27. Quoted in Melena Ryzik, "Heights Before Broadway," *New York Times*, March 14, 2008. www.nytimes.com/2008/03/14/theater/14heig.html.

28. "In the Heights: Chasing Broadway Dreams," PBS "Great Performances."

29. Miranda, "Pursuing the Muse."

30. Charles Isherwood, "From the Corner Bodega, the Music of Everyday Life," *New York Times*, February 9, 2007. www.nytimes.com/2007/02/09/theater/reviews/09heights.html.

31. Jeremy McCarter, "Something's Coming," *New York Magazine*, May 28, 2007. nymag.com/arts/theater/reviews/28107/.

32. "In the Heights: Chasing Broadway Dreams," PBS "Great Performances."

33. Charles Isherwood, "The View from Uptown: American Dreaming to a Latin Beat," *New York Times*, March 10, 2008. www.nytimes.com/2008/03/10/theater/reviews/10heig.html.

34. Quoted in Broadway.com Staff, "Thank You! The 2008 Tony Award Acceptance Speeches," Broadway.com, June 16, 2008. www.broadway.com/buzz/97439/thank-you-the-2008-tony-award-acceptance-speeches/.

35. Kenneth Jones, "Lin-Manuel Miranda to Leave *In the Heights* in February," *Playbill*, January 12, 2009. www.playbill. com/article/lin-manuel-miranda-to-leave-in-the-heights-in-february-com-156845.

36. Quoted in Browne, "Genius."

37. Quoted in Binelli, "'Hamilton' Creator Lin-Manuel Miranda."

Chapter Three: From One Great Project to the Next

38. Quoted in Anna Almendrala, "Lin-Manuel Miranda: It's 'No Accident' Hamilton Came to Me on Vacation," *Huffington Post*, June 23, 2016. www.huffingtonpost.com/entry/lin-manuel-miranda-says-its-no-accident-hamilton-inspiration-struck-on-vacation_us_576c136ee4b0b489bb0ca7c2.

39. Quoted in Binelli, "'Hamilton' Creator Lin-Manuel Miranda."

40. Quoted in Binelli, "'Hamilton' Creator Lin-Manuel Miranda."

41. Quoted in Binelli, "'Hamilton' Creator Lin-Manuel Miranda."

42. Quoted in Patricia Cohen, "Same City, New Story," *New York Times*, March 11, 2009. www.nytimes.com/2009/03/15/theater/15cohe.html?pagewanted=2.

43. Ben Brantley, "Our Gangs—Bernstein's 1957 Musical Revived at the Palace," *New York Times*, March 19, 2009. www.nytimes.com/2009/03/20/theater/reviews/20west.html?pagewanted=all.

44. "Lin-Manuel Miranda on Writing 'Sixteen Hot Bars' About Alexander Hamilton & Workshopping at the White House," Broadway.com, June 30, 2017. www.broadway.com/buzz/189066/lin-manuel-miranda-on-writing-sixteen-hot-bars-about-alexander-hamilton-workshopping-at-the-white-house/.

45. "Episode 9: Hamilton Part 1," Broadway Backstory podcast, 55:24, September 19, 2017. broadwaybackstory.libsyn.com/episode-9-hamilton-part-1.

46. Quoted in Browne, "Genius."

47. Quoted in Binelli, "'Hamilton' Creator Lin-Manuel Miranda."

48. Quoted in Binelli, "'Hamilton' Creator Lin-Manuel Miranda."

49. "Episode 9: Hamilton Part 1," Broadway Backstory Podcast.

50. Quoted in Mead, "All About the Hamiltons."

51. "Lin-Manuel Miranda in Conversation with Chris Jones," YouTube video.

52. Quoted in Browne, "Genius."

53. Quoted in BlackBook, "Lin-Manuel Miranda on 'Bring It On: The Musical,'" *BlackBook*, July 31, 2012. bbook.com/art/lin-manuel-miranda-on-bring-it-on-the-musical/.

54. "Episode 14: Bring It On: The Musical," Broadway Backstory podcast, 1:01:46, November 7, 2017. broadwaybackstory.libsyn.com/episode-14-bring-it-on-the-musical.

55. "Episode 9: Hamilton Part 1," Broadway Backstory Podcast.

56. Quoted in Adam Green, "Lin-Manuel Miranda's Groundbreaking Hip-Hop Musical, Hamilton, Hits Broadway," *Vogue*, June 24, 2015. www.vogue.com/article/hamilton-hip-hop-musical-broadway.

57. Quoted in Suzy Evans, "The Cabinet Behind Lin-Manuel Miranda's '*Hamilton*,'" *American Theatre*, August 6, 2015. www.americantheatre.org/2015/08/06/the-cabinet-behind-lin-manuel-mirandas-hamilton.

58. Quoted in Green, "Lin-Manuel Miranda's Groundbreaking Hip-Hop Musical."

59. Quoted in Evans, "The Cabinet."

60. Quoted in Jeff MacGregor, "Meet Lin-Manuel Miranda, the Genius Behind 'Hamilton,' Broadway's Newest Hit," *Smithsonian Magazine*, November 12, 2015. www.smithsonianmag.com/arts-culture/lin-manuel-miranda-ingenuity-awards-180957234/#lLzZo6JfbZUqJXSw.99.

61. Quoted in Browne, "Genius."

62. Quoted in Browne, "Genius."

Chapter Four: "Blow Us All Away"

63. "Episode 9: Hamilton Part 1," Broadway Backstory Podcast.

64. Quoted in Mead, "All About the Hamiltons."

65. Quoted in Suzy Evans, "How 'Hamilton' Found Its Groove," *American Theatre*, July 27, 2015. www.americantheatre. org/2015/07/27/how-hamilton-found-its-groove/.

66. Quoted in Evans, "How 'Hamilton' Found Its Groove."

67. Quoted in Paulson, "Lin-Manuel Miranda, Creator and Star."

68. Quoted in Paulson, "Lin-Manuel Miranda, Creator and Star."

69. L. V. Anderson, "Here Are the Original Casting Notices for *Hamilton* from Before It Was a Theater Legend," *Slate*, March 1, 2016. www.slate.com/blogs/browbeat/2016/03/01/hamilton_s_original_casting_notices_sum_up_each_character_from_before_they.html.

70. Quoted in Binelli, "'Hamilton' Creator Lin-Manuel Miranda."

71. Quoted in Binelli, "'Hamilton' Creator Lin-Manuel Miranda."

72. Quoted in Binelli, "'Hamilton' Creator Lin-Manuel Miranda."

73. Quoted in Binelli, "'Hamilton' Creator Lin-Manuel Miranda."

74. Quoted in Binelli, "'Hamilton' Creator Lin-Manuel Miranda."

75. Quoted in Binelli, "'Hamilton' Creator Lin-Manuel Miranda."

76. Quoted in Evans, "How 'Hamilton' Found Its Groove."

77. Quoted in Mead, "All About the Hamiltons."

78. Quoted in Evans, "The Cabinet."

79. Quoted in Michael Gioia, "Where It All Began—A Conversation with Lin-Manuel Miranda and His Father," *Playbill*, accessed on January 24, 2018. www.playbill.com/

article/where-it-all-begana-conversation-with-lin-manuel-miranda-and-his-father-com-353054.

80. Quoted in Mead, "All About the Hamiltons."

81. "Episode 10: Hamilton Part 2," Broadway Backstory podcast, 55:06, September 19, 2017. broadwaybackstory.libsyn.com/episode-10-hamilton-part-2.

82. Quoted in Mead, "All About the Hamiltons."

83. Quoted in Brian Hiatt, "'Hamilton': Meet the Man Behind Broadway's Hip-Hop Masterpiece," *Rolling Stone*, September 29, 2015. www.rollingstone.com/culture/features/hamilton-meet-the-man-behind-broadways-hip-hop-masterpiece-20150929.

84. Quoted in Binelli, "'Hamilton' Creator Lin-Manuel Miranda."

85. Quoted in Mead, "All About the Hamiltons."

86. Quoted in Mead, "All About the Hamiltons."

87. Quoted in Evans, "How 'Hamilton' Found Its Groove."

88. Ben Brantley, "Review: In 'Hamilton,' Lin-Manuel Miranda Forges Democracy Through Rap," *New York Times*, February 17, 2015. www.nytimes.com/2015/02/18/theater/review-in-hamilton-lin-manuel-miranda-forges-democracy-through-rap.html.

89. "Episode 10: Hamilton Part 2," Broadway Backstory podcast.

90. Quoted in Binelli, "'Hamilton' Creator Lin-Manuel Miranda."

91. Quoted in Browne, "Genius."

92. "Episode 10: Hamilton Part 2," Broadway Backstory podcast.

93. Quoted in Green, "Lin-Manuel Miranda's Groundbreaking Hip-Hop Musical."

94. "Episode 10: Hamilton Part 2," Broadway Backstory podcast.

95. Quoted in Michael Gioia, "Hundreds Mob the First *Hamilton*

Lottery—See Which Broadway Star Won!," *Playbill*, July 14, 2015. www.playbill.com/article/hundreds-mob-the-first-hamilton-lottery-see-which-broadway-star-won-com-353241.

96. "Episode 10: Hamilton Part 2," Broadway Backstory podcast.

97. Peter Marks, "'Hamilton': Making Ecstatic History," *Washington Post*, August 6, 2015. www.washingtonpost.com/entertainment/theater_dance/hamilton-making-ecstatic-history/2015/08/06/6bc85fb4-3b72-11e5-8e98-115a3cf-7d7ae_story.html?utm_term=.7e094f91d0db.

98. Quoted in MacGregor, "Meet Lin-Manuel Miranda."

99. Quoted in Evans, "How 'Hamilton' Found Its Groove."

100. Quoted in Hiatt, "'Hamilton': Meet the Man."

101. Quoted in MacGregor, "Meet Lin-Manuel Miranda."

102. "Lin-Manuel Miranda," MacArthur Foundation, accessed on January 24, 2018. www.macfound.org/fellows/941/.

103. "Hamilton—Best Musical Theater Album—58th Grammys," YouTube video, 1:36, posted by Recording Academy / Grammys, February 15, 2016. www.youtube.com/watch?v=C7tkP3emR9I.

104. Quoted in Robert Viagas, "*Hamilton* Wins 2016 Pulitzer Prize; Miranda Reacts," *Playbill*, April 18, 2016. www.playbill.com/article/hamilton-wins-2016-pulitzer-prize-com-347196.

105. "Episode 10: Hamilton Part 2," Broadway Backstory podcast.

106. "Lin-Manuel Miranda's Sonnet from the Tony Awards," *New York Times*, June 12, 2016. www.nytimes.com/2016/06/13/theater/lin-manuel-mirandas-sonnet-from-the-tony-awards.html.

107. "Lin-Manuel Miranda in Conversation with Chris Jones," YouTube video.

Chapter Five: How Far He Will Go

108. Quoted in Daniel Kreps, "Watch 'Hamilton' Cast Perform at the White House," *Rolling Stone*, March 14, 2016. www.rollingstone.com/music/news/watch-hamilton-cast-perform-at-the-white-house-20160314.

109. Quoted in Michael Paulson, "Lin-Manuel Miranda Confirms He's Leaving 'Hamilton' on July 9," *New York Times*, June 16, 2016. www.nytimes.com/2016/06/17/theater/lin-manuel-miranda-confirms-hes-leaving-hamilton-on-july-9.html.

110. Quoted in Michael Paterniti, "Lin-Manuel Miranda Is Ready for His Next Act," *GQ*, September 20, 2016. www.gq.com/story/lin-manuel-miranda-profile-gq-cover.

111. Quoted in Isabella Biedenharn, "Making *The Hamilton Mixtape*: Lin-Manuel Miranda Explains the Stories Behind the Songs," *Entertainment Weekly*, November 30, 2016. ew.com/music/2016/11/30/hamilton-mixtape-lin-manuel-miranda-songs/.

112. Quoted in Biedenharn, "Making *The Hamilton Mixtape*."

113. Quoted in Melinda Newman, "Lin-Manuel Miranda on 'Moana' Music, Potential EGOT Status and Staying Positive Under Trump," *Hollywood Reporter*, January 11, 2017. www.hollywoodreporter.com/news/lin-manuel-miranda-moana-music-potential-egot-status-staying-positive-under-trump-963551.

114. Quoted in Newman, "Lin-Manuel Miranda on 'Moana' Music."

115. Quoted in Newman, "Lin-Manuel Miranda on 'Moana' Music."

116. Quoted in Lindsay Kimble, "Lin-Manuel Miranda's Mother Joins Him on the Oscars Red Carpet: 'I Knew He Would Be Here One Day,'" *People*, February 26, 2017. people.com/awards/oscars-2017-lin-manuel-miranda-mom-red-carpet/.

117. Quoted in Marc Snetiker, "How Lin-Manuel Miranda's *Mary Poppins* Sequel Character Connects to Dick Van Dyke," *Entertainment Weekly*, June 8, 2017. ew.com/movies/2017/06/08/mary-poppins-returns-lin-manuel-miranda-dick-van-dyke/.

118. Quoted in Newman, "Lin-Manuel Miranda on 'Moana' Music."

119. Lin-Manuel Miranda, "Lin-Manuel Miranda's Personal Plea for Puerto Rico Hurricane Relief (Guest Column)," *Hollywood Reporter*, September 26, 2017. www.hollywoodreporter.com/news/lin-manuel-mirandas-emotional-plea-puerto-rico-hurricane-relief-guest-column-1043170.

120. Quoted in Chris Jones, "'Hamilton's' Lin-Manuel Miranda and the Terrifying Urgency of Fame," *Chicago Tribune*, September 7, 2016. www.chicagotribune.com/entertainment/theater/hamilton/ct-fall-preview-2016-hamilton-theater-feature-ae-0911-20160907-column.html.

121. Quoted in Lauren Rubenstein, "Lin-Manuel Miranda '02 Delivers Commencement Address," Wesleyan University, May 24, 2015. newsletter.blogs.wesleyan.edu/2015/05/24/mirandacommencementspeech/.

122. Quoted in Hiatt, "'Hamilton': Meet the Man."

123. Quoted in Evans, "How 'Hamilton' Found Its Groove."

124. Video embedded in Devan Coggan, "See the *Hamilton-Moana* Mash-Up that Made Lin-Manuel Miranda Cry on the Oscars Red Carpet," *Entertainment Weekly*, 1:35, February 26, 2017. ew.com/awards/2017/02/26/oscars-2017-lin-manuel-miranda-cries-on-the-red-carpet-hamilton-moana-mash-up/.

Lin-Manuel Miranda Year by Year

1980

Lin-Manuel Miranda is born on January 16.

1998

Miranda graduates from Hunter College High School. He starts college at Wesleyan University.

2000

The 80-minute, 1-act version of *In the Heights* is performed at Wesleyan.

2002

Miranda graduates from Wesleyan University.

2007

In the Heights opens Off-Broadway, with Miranda in a leading role as Usnavi.

2008

In the Heights opens on Broadway, and Miranda makes his Broadway debut. *In the Heights* wins four Tony Awards including Miranda winning for Best Original Score. It also won Best Choreography, Best Orchestrations, and Best Musical. Miranda takes a vacation and has the idea for *Hamilton* while reading Ron Chernow's book.

2009

In the Heights wins a Grammy Award for its cast album. Miranda finishes his run in the Broadway cast of *In the Heights*. The revival of *West Side Story* opens on Broadway. Miranda performs the first 16 bars of *Hamilton* at the White House. He begins work on *Bring It On: The Musical*. Miranda and Vanessa Nadal get engaged. Miranda is nominated for a Pulitzer Prize for *In the Heights*.

2010

Miranda marries Vanessa Nadal. The recording of the *West Side Story* revival wins a Grammy Award.

2011

West Side Story closes on Broadway. *In the Heights* closes on Broadway; Miranda performs in the last two weeks of the run. *Bring It On* premieres in Atlanta, Georgia. Miranda performs "My Shot" at a benefit.

2012

Bring It On opens and closes on Broadway. Miranda and others perform parts of *Hamilton* at the *American Songbook* series. Readings of *Hamilton* begin. The revival of *Working*, which Miranda wrote new songs for, opens Off-Broadway. Miranda films a part on the TV show *Do No Harm*.

2013

Miranda, Lacamoire, and Kail go to Vassar College to work exclusively on *Hamilton* for a short period of time. Miranda agrees to start working with the Public Theater and Oskar Eustis.

2014

Miranda wins an Emmy with Tom Kitt for a song written for the 67th Tony Awards. Sebastian Miranda is born. *In the Heights* opens in London, and Miranda wins an Olivier Award for it. The Freestyle Love Supreme TV show airs. Miranda stars in *Tick, Tick...Boom!*. Workshops for *Hamilton* occur at the Public Theater.

2015

Hamilton opens Off-Broadway and moves to Broadway in July. Miranda receives a MacArthur Foundation Award, three Drama Desk Awards, and more. Miranda contributes music to *Star Wars: The Force Awakens*. He gives the commencement address at Wesleyan University.

2016

Miranda wins the Pulitzer Prize in Drama for *Hamilton*. *Hamilton* wins a Grammy Award for its cast album. Miranda is nominated for three Tony Awards and wins Best Score and Best Book of a Musical; *Hamilton* wins another eight Tonys, including Best Musical. The cast of *Hamilton* performs at the White House. Miranda releases "Love Make the World Go Round" with Jennifer Lopez in tribute to the victims of the Pulse nightclub shooting. Miranda leaves the cast of *Hamilton*. *The Hamilton Mixtape* is released. *Moana*, with music from Miranda, is released.

2017

Miranda receives an Oscar nomination for his song "How Far I'll Go" from *Moana*. Miranda releases "Almost Like Praying" to raise money for Puerto Rican hurricane relief efforts. *Hamilton* begins its national tour in Los Angeles. *Hamilton* opens in London. The Miranda family is honored at the Imagen Awards. Miranda is nominated for a Grammy for "How Far I'll Go." He begins releasing "Hamildrops."

2018

Miranda and his wife welcome their second child, Francisco, on February 2. *Mary Poppins Returns* is released, starring Miranda.

For More Information

Books

Boehme, Gerry. *How Hamilton Made It to the Stage*. New York, NY: Cavendish Square, 2018.
Boehme's book allows the reader to learn more about the process of *Hamilton's* creation.

Grode, Eric. *The Book of Broadway: The 150 Definitive Plays and Musicals*. Minneapolis, MN: Voyageur Press, 2017.
Explore some of the best-known Broadway shows of all time in this comprehensive book.

Hudes, Quiara Alegría. *In the Heights: The Complete Book and Lyrics of the Broadway Musical*. Milwaukee, WI: Applause Theatre & Cinema Books, 2013.
This volume includes every word of *In the Heights* as it is performed on stage, from dialogue to song lyrics.

Miranda, Lin-Manuel, and Jeremy McCarter. *Hamilton: The Revolution*. New York, NY: Grand Central Publishing, 2016.
This book presents the lyrics and story of *Hamilton* along with Miranda's annotations, thoughts, and images from the show.

Prince, Harold. *Sense of Occasion*. Milwaukee, WI: Applause Theatre and Cinema Books, 2017.
One of the most famous Broadway directors of all time shares insight into the business of Broadway and the many Tony Award–winning shows he has been part of.

Websites

Broadway.com
(www.broadway.com)
Learn all about the most recent shows on Broadway, how tickets can be bought, and other news about Broadway stars, shows, and more.

Camp Broadway
(www.campbroadway.com)
Camp Broadway has information on Broadway careers and programs that can help those interested in a career get started.

Hamilton
(www.hamiltonbroadway.com)
The official *Hamilton* website has information on where *Hamilton* is playing across the United States and abroad.

Lin-Manuel Miranda
(www.linmanuel.com)
Miranda's personal website keeps fans up-to-date with news about his latest projects.

Lin-Manuel Miranda on Facebook
(www.facebook.com/Lin-Manuel-Miranda-156195014444203)
Follow Lin-Manuel Miranda's official Facebook page for updates straight from the star.

Lin-Manuel Miranda on Twitter
(twitter.com/Lin_Manuel)
Follow @Lin_Manuel on Twitter and get the inside scoop on Miranda's life, interests, and latest projects.

Playbill
(www.playbill.com)
The official *Playbill* website has the latest theater news from Broadway and beyond.

Index

Picture Credits

Cover, p. 71 Theo Wargo/Getty Images for Tony Awards Productions; pp. 10, 56 (bottom) Walter McBride/WireImage/ Getty Images; p. 12 GV Cruz/WireImage/Getty Images; p. 14 Santiago Felipe/Getty Images; p. 17 Janette Pellegrini/WireImage/ Getty Images; p. 21 Chelsea Lauren/Getty Images for the Pantages Theatre; p. 22 Kevin Yatarola/Getty Images; p. 24 Walter McBride/ Corbis via Getty Images; p. 26 Scott Gries/Getty Images; p. 30 Steven A Henry/WireImage/Getty Images; p. 32 Theo Wargo/WireImage/ Getty Images; p. 37 Leigh Vogel/Getty Images for National Archives Foundation; p. 39 Bruce Glikas/FilmMagic/Getty Images; p. 41 Ron Sachs-Pool via Getty Images; p. 42 Andy Kropa/Getty Images; p. 45 J. Countess/WireImage/Getty Images; p. 47 Stuart C. Wilson/Getty Images; p. 48 Monica Schipper/Getty Images; p. 54 Theo Wargo/Getty Images; p. 56 (top) John Paul Filo/ CBS via Getty Images; p. 58 Munin2005/Wikimedia Commons; p. 62 Nicholas Hunt/Getty Images; p. 63 Scott Dudelson/Getty Images; p. 65 Joseph M. Arseneau/Shutterstock.com; p. 66 Matt Winkelmeyer/Getty Images; p. 73 NICHOLAS KAMM/AFP/ Getty Images; p. 75 Johnny Nunez/WireImage/Getty Images; p. 76 Kathy Hutchins/Shutterstock.com; p. 79 Raymond Hall/ GC Images/Getty Images; p. 80 Paul Morigi/Getty Images; p. 81 Presley Ann/Getty Images; p. 82 David M. Benett/Dave Benett/ Getty Images.

About the Author

Kristen Rajczak Nelson is the associate editorial director of Gareth Stevens Publishing and the author of hundreds of educational children's books. She has a bachelor's degree in English from Gannon University and a master's degree in Arts Journalism from the S.I. Newhouse School of Public Communications at Syracuse University, with a concentration in theater criticism. Kristen grew up listening to *Les Misérables* and *Phantom of the Opera*. Today, she continues to love listening to and taking in musicals of local, touring, and Broadway productions. She lives outside Buffalo, New York, with her husband.